The SURRENDER of
NAPOLEON

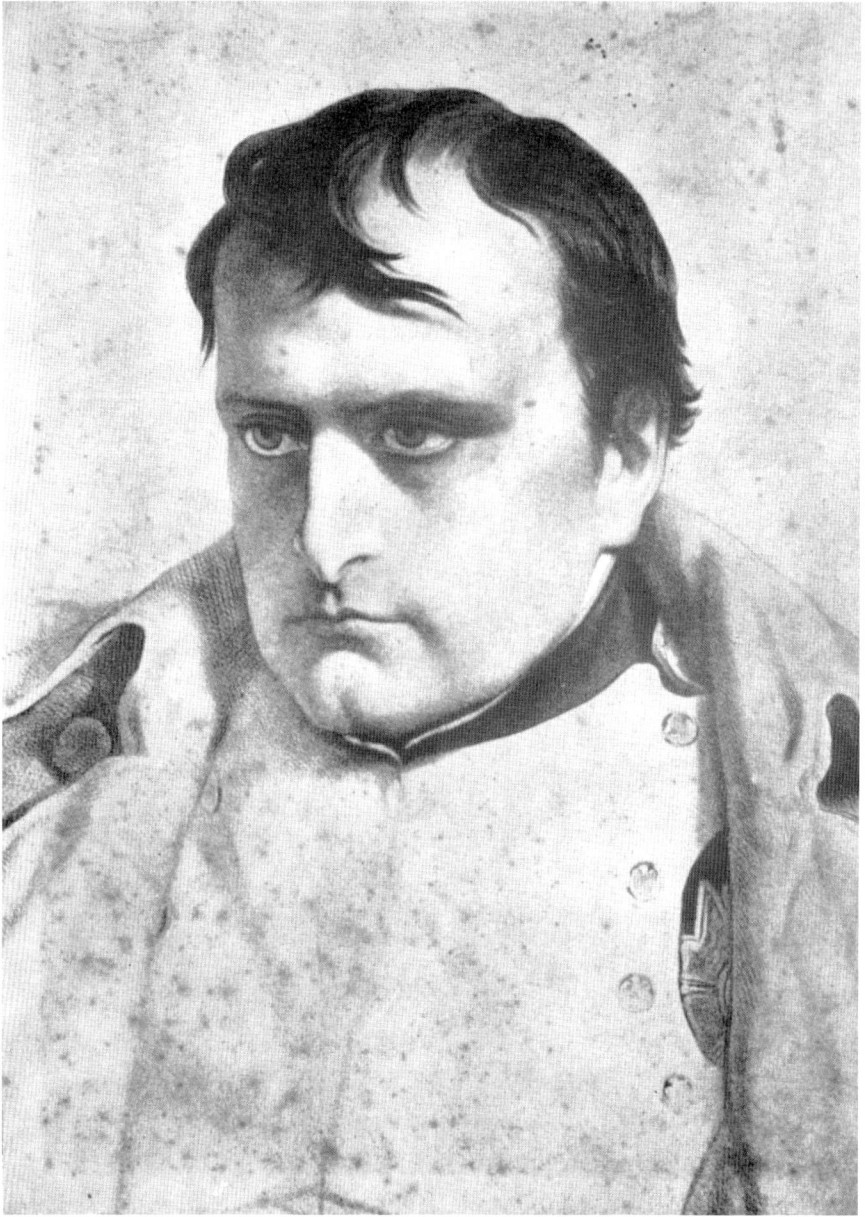

A portrait of Napoleon in 1815.

The SURRENDER of NAPOLEON

THE CAPTURE OF THE EMPEROR
AFTER WATERLOO

FREDERICK LEWIS MAITLAND

FONTHILL

Learn more about Fonthill Media. Join our mailing list to find out about our latest titles and special offers at: www.fonthillmedia.com

Fonthill Media Limited
Fonthill Media LLC
www.fonthillmedia.com
office@fonthillmedia.com

This edition first published in the United Kingdom 2013 and the United States of America 2014

Copyright © In this edition Fonthill Media 2013

ISBN 978-1-78155-176-9

Typeset in Sabon 10/14
Printed and bound in England
 twitter.com/fonthillmedia facebook.com/fonthillmedia

The Battle of Waterloo, 18 June 1815.

Contents

Lucien Bonaparte, (1775-1840). A portrait by Francois-Xavier Fabre painted after 1800.

The King of Rome, Napoléon II; Napoléon Francis Joseph Charles Bonaparte; an engraving after a portrait by Sir Thomas Lawrence.

Introduction to the 2013 Edition

After the Battle of Waterloo (18 June 1815), the remaining remnants of the French army retreated to Paris, arriving there on the 21st. Napoleon still clung to the hope of concerting national resistance; but the temper of the chambers and of the public in general precluded any such attempt. Napoleon and his brother Lucien were almost alone in believing that by dissolving the chambers and declaring Napoleon dictator they could save France from the armies of the powers now converging on Paris. Even Davout, minister of war, advised Napoleon that the destinies of France rested solely with the chambers. Clearly, it was time to safeguard what remained; and that could best be done under Talleyrand's shield of legitimacy. Napoleon eventually recognised the truth. When Lucien pressed him to "dare", he replied, "Alas, I have dared only too much already". On 22 June 1815 he abdicated in favour of his son, Napoléon Francis Joseph Charles Bonaparte, well knowing that it was a formality, as his four-year-old son was in Austria. On 25 June he received from Fouché, his former police chief, and now the president of the newly appointed provisional government, an intimation that he must leave Paris. He retired first to Malmaison, the former home of Joséphine. On 29 June, on hearing of the near approach of the Prussians, who had orders to seize him, dead or alive, he retired westwards toward Rochefort, accompanied by a loyal entourage, from whence he hoped to reach the United States on board an awaiting French frigate whose officers and crew remained loyal to him. The presence of blockading Royal Navy warships with orders to prevent his escape forestalled this plan. Finally, unable to remain in France or escape from it, and not wishing to fall into the hands of vindictive Bourbons, he surrendered himself to Captain Maitland of HMS *Bellerophon*.

.   .   .   .   .

Sir Frederick Lewis Maitland, (1777-1839), was the third son of Captain Frederick Lewis Maitland (1730-1786), sixth son of Charles, sixth earl of Lauderdale. Maitland's father, the godson of Frederick Louis, Prince of Wales, commanded with distinction the *Lively* in 1760, the *Elizabeth* in 1778, and served under Rodney in 1782. Between 1763 and 1775 he commanded the royal yacht. He was promoted rear-admiral in 1786, but died before the news reached him. Maitland's mother was Margaret Dick (d. 1825), heir in tail general to James Crichton, Viscount Frendraught, who was heir of the family of Makgill of Rankeilour.

Frederick Maitland's career and general biography is covered in the first half of this book. Suffice it to say in this introduction, that he was fortunate enough to be the Royal Navy officer in the right place at the right time. In 1813 and 1814 Frederick Maitland commanded the *Goliath* (58 guns) on the Halifax and West Indian stations, and in November 1814 was appointed to the *Boyne* (98 guns) under orders for North America. At the beginning of 1815 he was collecting a fleet of transports and merchant ships in Cork harbour, but a succession of strong westerly winds prevented his sailing, until, on the news of Napoleon's return from Elba, his orders were countermanded, and he was appointed to the *Bellerophon* (74 guns), in which he sailed from Plymouth on 24 May under the immediate orders of Sir Henry Hotham. Maitland, as well as Hotham, had a long experience of the Bay of Biscay, and the *Bellerophon* was stationed off Rochefort to keep watch on the ships of war there. On 28 June the news of Waterloo reached Maitland, and on the 30th a letter from Bordeaux warned him that Napoleon would attempt to escape from there to the United States of America. Maitland, however, with good sense considered Napoleon would more probably make for Rochefort; and though he sent two small craft, one to Bordeaux and the other to Arcachon, he himself, in the *Bellerophon*, remained off Rochefort. Hotham, in the *Superb*, was in Quiberon Bay, and frigates, corvettes, and brigs kept watch along the whole extent of the coast. Hotham ordered Maitland that if he intercepted Napoleon he should take him to England.

On 10 July 1815 negotiations with Frederick Maitland were opened on behalf of Napoleon, who had then reached Rochefort. This was a tense time for Maitland, for a misjudgment or error could have proved decisive and there were genuine possibilities that the French frigate, still loyal to Napoleon, could have slipped past the Royal Navy blockade. Maitland rejected the proposal that Napoleon should be allowed to sail to the United States, but instead offered to take him to England. Napoleon was under the delusion that he might be allowed, by the British Government, to live the quiet life of a country gentleman in England and Maitland did nothing to dispel that belief. After four anxious days, Napoleon, with his staff and servants, embarked on the *Bellerophon* on 15 July. On 24 July the ship reached Torbay; thence she was ordered round to Plymouth to await the decision of the government. She put to sea again on 4 August, and on the 7th, off Berry Head, Napoleon was removed to the *Northumberland*.

To counteract misrepresentation, Maitland wrote for his friends a detailed Narrative of Napoleon's time on the *Bellerophon*, which he subsequently published in 1826, and this forms the basis for this much revised text which was published in 1904.

·   ·   ·   ·   ·

Sir Walter Scott showed a great interest in the original work, but nothing happened for a long time after the initial limited edition of 1826. After Sir Frederick Maitland's death in 1839 his papers passed into the hands of Lady Maitland, who life-rented his property of Lindores in Fife until her death in 1865. They then passed with the property to Sir Frederick's nephew, Captain James Maitland, RN, and on his death to his brother, Rear-Admiral Lewis Maitland, from whom they then descended to his son, Frederick Lewis Maitland.

Realising the on-going interest, Frederick Maitland junior arranged for the papers of his great-uncle to be edited by William Kirk Dickson, (1860-1949), and this was published in 1904.

The detail supplied by Maitland provides a vital historical record of those bitter days; a period for Napoleon where he attempted to come to terms with his total downfall. He clung to the hope that he could prevail upon the Prince of Wales to allow him to retire to a modest country estate 'reasonably close to London'. One of the appendices, the extract from *The Memoirs of an Aristocrat*, by George Home, (who, in 1815, was a midshipman on board HMS *Bellerophon*), provides an even better sense of the poignancy; describing with feeling Napoleon's six or so hours on the poop-deck of *Bellerophon*, seated on a gun saddle with his pocket glass looking at the island of Ushant and the receding coast of Brittany.

Napoleon's desire to speak to the Prince of Wales had good logic, and had he succeeded the outcome may have been different. Government ministers, however, knew the Prince better and ensured that they blocked any such interview. Lord Keith, after his short interview with Napoleon realised he was a man who could emanate charm and made an interesting unguarded comment as reported by Maitland: 'Lord Keith appears to have formed a very high opinion of the fascination of his conversation, and expressed it very emphatically to me, after he had seen him: speaking of his wish for an interview with the Prince Regent, "D—n the fellow," he said, "if he had obtained an interview with his Royal Highness, in half an hour they would have been the best friends in England.""

It was not to be. Government ministers were paranoid about Napoleon and sent him to St Helena with a preposterously large military and naval guard, and there Napoleon died on 5 May 1821.

·   ·   ·   ·   ·

This edition is effectively the 1904 edition in modern typography with a few end notes added and additional illustrations. The first quarter of the text is an extended biography of Maitland, followed by Maitland's own narrative as edited by Dickson. At the end, a few appendices are provided as selected by William Dickson.

Memoir of Sir Frederick Lewis Maitland

The name of Sir Frederick Lewis Maitland has found a permanent place in history as that of the captor of Napoleon. Apart from the rare piece of good fortune which befell him in the Basque Roads in July 1815, his distinguished career of public service entitles him to an honourable place in the records of the British Navy.

He was the third son of Captain the Hon. Frederick Lewis Maitland, RN, and was born at Rankeilour in Fife on 7 September 1777. His father, Captain Maitland, was the sixth son of Charles, sixth Earl of Lauderdale, grand-nephew of Charles II's famous minister, and was godson to Frederick Lewis, Prince of Wales, the eldest son of George II. He held various naval commands with distinction, served under Rodney in 1782, and between 1763 and 1775 commanded the royal yacht. He died in 1786, having been promoted rear-admiral just before his death. Maitland's mother, Margaret Dick, was the heiress of the family of Makgill of Rankeilour. The estates of that family were ultimately inherited by her eldest son, Charles Maitland.

Young Maitland entered his father's profession at a very early age. He served as a midshipman, first under Captain George Duff in the *Martin* sloop-of-war, and afterwards with the Hon. Robert Forbes in the *Southampton* frigate, in which he was present at Lord Howe's great victory off Ushant on 1 June 1794,—the "glorious First of June." On 5 April 1795, he was promoted to the rank of lieutenant, and appointed to the *Andromeda*, of 32 guns. From the *Andromeda* he was removed to the *Venerable*, the flagship of Admiral Duncan in the North Sea. In April 1797 he went out to the Mediterranean to join Lord St Vincent.

St Vincent had been a friend of his father's, and had promised to promote him as opportunity should occur. The flagship had her full complement of officers, so Maitland was appointed first lieutenant of the *Kingfisher*, a brig mounting 18 six-pounders and commanded by the Hon. Charles Herbert

Pierrepont, afterwards Earl Manvers. In her he was present at the capture of four French privateers. With one of these, the *Betsey*, of 16 guns, a severe action was fought. When the prize-money for her capture was distributed, the crew of the Kingfisher subscribed £50 to present Maitland with a sword in recognition of his conduct.

Pierrepont was promoted to post rank in December 1798, and appointed to the *Spartiate*, one of Nelson's prizes taken at the Nile. A few days after his departure the *Kingfisher*, under Maitland's command, was leaving the Tagus, when she grounded on Lisbon bar and became a total wreck. Maitland was tried by court-martial at Gibraltar, and acquitted of all blame in connection with her loss. Immediately after his trial he was appointed flag-lieutenant to Lord St Vincent.

On 23 June 1799, the French and Spanish fleets effected a junction at Cartagena, and in the following month they retired from the Mediterranean and took refuge in Brest. They passed the Straits of Gibraltar on 7 July when Maitland had an adventure which is described in Tucker's *Memoirs of Earl St Vincent*.

"It is," he says, "an as yet untold anecdote of the presence of mind and courage of one of the highest-minded characters that ever adorned the British Navy, the late Rear-Admiral Sir Frederick Maitland.

"At this period that gallant officer was Lord St Vincent's flag-lieutenant; and when the fleets were first descried, Johnny Gilpin, as his lordship used to call him, was sent to order the *Penelope*, a little hired cutter, to go, count, and dodge them. The lieutenant commanding the cutter was found too ill to utter an order. But Mr Maitland, well knowing his Chief, and that this was service which must be done, at once assumed the command, and got the vessel under weigh. He stood over to Ceuta. The night was so pitchy dark and so calm that the cutter was unperceived by the enemy, and yet so close among them that the words of command in French and Spanish could be distinctly heard. At daybreak she was about gunshot distance from the whole Spanish fleet. When they saw her their admiral signalled a number of launches to tow a brig of 14 guns to attack her, but on their arrival within shot from the little *Penelope*, the reception she astonished them with was so spirited that the enemy dropped astern again and retired; and a faint hope of escape appeared, for, there being no wind, the cutter's boats were kept ahead all the forenoon, towing to the southward. Then every ship in that mighty fleet, except one frigate, actually turned their heads to the southward to give chase to the cutter. But the frigate stood to the northward, and as the afternoon's westerly breeze got up, it brought her down under studding-sails near the *Penelope*, before the air had reached her. When she was within cable's length, the frigate opened her broadside fire. Mr Maitland told the cutter's crew to lie down upon the deck till the frigate had discharged all her guns. The men lay down very smartly; but when ordered to rise, splice the topsail braces, and get the vessel's head about, not a man of them would stir. 'Fighting,' they said, 'was not their employ; they were not hired for it, and, should they lose a limb, there was no provision for them;' and thus the frigate now renewing her fire, the little *Penelope* was taken.

"To the honour of the Spanish admiral it must be added, that, having witnessed this bravery and heard that it was Lord St Vincent's flag-lieutenant that had displayed it, he sent Mr Maitland in a cartel to Gibraltar, declaring him free without exchange."

Tucker, who wrote in 1844, was not quite correct in saying that the anecdote was "as yet untold." It had been given long before in Marshall's *Naval Biography*. Marshall mentions, among other details, that "the *Penelope* had on board a sum of money intended for Minorca, which it was not deemed advisable to remove, under the pressing urgency for her immediate departure from Gibraltar. When her crew found there was no chance of escape from the combined fleets, they made an attempt to plunder the treasure, which Lieutenant Maitland most honourably and successfully resisted, alleging that as public property it was the lawful prize of the captors."

Lord St Vincent returned to England in August 1799, accompanied by Maitland. On reaching Portsmouth he heard of an explosion of shells which had taken place in May on board the *Theseus*, 74, resulting in the death of her commander, Captain Ralph Willet Miller. A vacancy had thus occurred in the Mediterranean before the admiral quitted that station. He used his privilege as commander-in-chief and promoted Maitland to the rank of commander in the *Cameleon* sloop-of-war, the promotion to date from 14 June. Maitland at once went out to join his new ship, which was then on the coast of Egypt under Sir Sidney Smith. After the signing of the convention of El Arish he was sent home with despatches. He returned and regained his ship, in which he made several captures.

On 10 December 1800, he was appointed by Lord Keith to the *Wassenaar*, 64. As she was then lying at Malta unfit for service, he obtained permission to accompany Sir Ralph Abercromby's expedition to Egypt.

The fleet anchored in Aboukir Bay on 2 March 1801. On the 8th, Abercromby effected a landing in face of a large and strongly posted French force. To Maitland fell the duty of commanding the armed launches employed to cover the landing. The enemy were driven from their positions, and retired towards Alexandria with the loss of seven guns. Abercromby at once followed them up, and advanced on the neck of sand lying between the sea and the Lake of Aboukir, leaving a distance of about four miles between the English and French camps. On the 13th he again attacked the French, and forced them back upon their lines before Alexandria. The right flank of the British force rested on the sea, the left on the Lake of Aboukir, and the flanks were covered by a naval flotilla, the boats on the sea being under Maitland's command, and those on the lake under that of Captain James Hillyar. Seven days later Sir Sidney Smith, who commanded the naval battalion serving on shore, received from a friendly Arab sheikh a letter informing him that it was General Menou's intention to attack the British camp next morning. The news was thought too good to be true, as in a few days Abercromby would have been compelled to attack the lines of Alexandria under every tactical disadvantage. It was, however, confirmed, and on the 21st of March the battle of Alexandria was fought, the fate of Egypt was decided, and Abercromby received his death-wound. Maitland again covered the British right flank from the sea. In the detailed plan of the battle given in Sir Robert Wilson's *History of the British Expedition to Egypt*, Maitland's flotilla is shown a little to the west of the ruins of Nicopolis, in a position to enfilade the French attack. For his services on the 8th, 13th, and 21st Maitland received the thanks of the naval and military commanders-in-chief, and on 22 March, the day after the battle, Sir Sidney Smith wrote to Lord Keith warmly commending Maitland's conduct.

Maitland's post commission was confirmed by the Admiralty on the day of the battle of Alexandria. In the ensuing month he was appointed to the *Dragon*, 74, and shortly afterwards to the *Carrère*, a French 40-gun frigate taken near Elba. He remained in command of her in the Mediterranean till the Peace of Amiens.

The *Carrère* was paid off on 4 October 1802. Eleven days afterwards Maitland was appointed by Lord St Vincent to the *Loire*, a fine 46-gun frigate. War broke out again on 18 May 1803, and the *Loire* started on a brilliant career of captures, which included the 10-gun brig *Venteux*, cut out from under the Isle of Bas by two of the *Loire*'s boats, the *Braave* privateer, and the 30-gun frigate *Blonde*, captured in August 1804 after a pursuit of twenty hours and a desperate running fight.

An official letter written by Maitland in June 1805, gives us a vivid glimpse of frigate service in the old days:—

Captain Maitland to Rear-Admiral Drury, Cork.

Loire, Muros Road, Spain,
June 4, 1805.

Sir,—Being informed that there was a French privateer of 26 guns fitting out at Muros, and nearly ready for sea, it struck me, from my recollection of the bay (having been in it formerly, when lieutenant of the *Kingfisher*), as being practicable either to bring her out or destroy her with the ship I have the honour to command. I accordingly prepared yesterday evening for engaging at anchor, and appointed Mr Yeo, with Lieutenants Mallock and Douglas, of the marines, and Mr Clinch, master's-mate, to head the boarders and marines, amounting, officers included, to 50 men (being all that could be spared from anchoring the ship and working the guns), in landing and storming the fort, though I then had no idea its strength was so great as it has proved. At nine this morning, on the sea-breeze setting in, I stood for the bay in the ship, the men previously prepared, being in the boats ready to shove off. On hauling close round the point of the road, a small battery of 2 guns opened a fire on the ship; a few shot were returned; but perceiving it would annoy us considerably, from its situation, I desired Mr Yeo to push on shore and spike the guns; reminding the men of its being the anniversary of their Sovereign's birth, and that, for his sake, as well as their own credit, their utmost exertions must be used. Though such an injunction was unnecessary, it had a great effect in animating and raising the spirits of the people. As the ship drew in, and more fully opened the bay, I perceived a very long corvette, of 26 ports, apparently nearly ready for sea, and a large brig of 20 ports, in a state of fitting; but neither of them firing, led me to conclude they had not their guns on board, and left no other object to occupy my attention but a heavy fort, which at this moment opened to our view, within less than a quarter of a mile, and began a wonderfully well-directed fire, almost every shot taking place in the hull. Perceiving that, by standing further on, more guns would be brought to bear upon us, without our being enabled to near the fort so much as I wished, I ordered the helm to be put down; and when, from the way she had, we had gained an advantageous position, anchored with a spring, and commenced firing. Although I have but little doubt that, before long, we should have silenced the fort, yet, from the specimen they gave us, and being completely embrasured, it must have cost us many lives, and caused great injury to the ship, had not Mr Yeo's gallantry and good conduct soon put an end to their fire.

I must now revert to him and the party under his command. Having landed under the small battery on the point, it was instantly abandoned; but hardly had he time to spike the guns, when, at the distance of a quarter of a mile, he perceived a regular fort, ditched, and with a gate, which the enemy (fortunately never suspecting our landing) had neglected to secure, open a fire upon the ship. Without waiting for orders he pushed forward, and was opposed at the inner gate by the Governor, with such troops as were in the town, and the crews of the French privateers. From the testimony of the prisoners as well as our own men, it appears that Mr Yeo was the first who entered the fort, with one blow laid the Governor dead at his feet, and broke his own sabre in two. The other officers were despatched by such officers and men of ours as were most advanced, and the narrowness of the gate would permit to push forward. The remainder instantly fled to the further end of the fort, and from the ship we could perceive many of them leap from the embrasures upon the rocks, a height of above 25 feet. Such as laid down their arms received quarter. . . .

The instant the Union was displayed at the fort, I sent and took possession of the enemies' vessels in the Road, consisting of the *Confiance*, French ship privateer, pierced for 26 twelves and nines, none of which, however, were on board; the *Bélier*, French privateer brig, pierced for 20 eighteen-pounder carronades; and a Spanish merchant brig in ballast. I then hoisted a flag of truce, and sent to inform the inhabitants of the town, that if they would deliver up such stores of the ship as were on shore, there would be no further molestation. The proposal was thankfully agreed to. I did not, however, think it advisable to allow the people to remain long enough to embark the guns, there being a large body of troops in the vicinity. A great many small vessels are in the bay, and hauled up on the beach. None of them having cargoes of any value, I conceive it an act of inhumanity to deprive the poorer inhabitants of the means of gaining their livelihood, and shall not molest them. On inspecting the brig, as she had only the lower rigging overhead, and was not in a state of forwardness, I found it impracticable to bring her away, and therefore set fire to her: she is now burnt to the water's edge. I cannot conclude my letter without giving the portion of credit that is their due to the officers and men on board the ship. They conducted themselves with the greatest steadiness and coolness; and although under a heavy fire, pointed their guns with the utmost precision, there being hardly a shot that did not take effect. . . . It is but fair at the same time to state that, much to the credit of the ship's company, the Bishop and one of the principal inhabitants of the town came off to express their gratitude for the orderly behaviour of the people, there not being one instance of pillage; and to make offer of every refreshment the place affords.

I am now waiting for the land breeze to carry us out, having already recalled the officers and men from the fort, the guns being spiked and thrown over the parapet, the carriages rendered unserviceable, and the embrasures, with part of the fort, blown up.

I have the honour to be, &c.,

Fred. L. Maitland

On 27 June 1805, the Common Council of the City of London voted him their thanks for his distinguished conduct in Muros Bay. The Committee of the Patriotic Fund at Lloyd's presented him with a sword, and on 18 October he received the freedom of the city of Cork in recognition of his exertions for the protection of Irish trade. In the following winter the *Loire* had a narrow escape. Marshall thus describes the incident:

> On the 13th Dec. 1805, the *Loire*, accompanied by the *Alcmene* frigate, fell in with the Rochefort squadron, consisting of six sail of the line, three frigates, and three corvettes. Maitland immediately sent the *Alcmene* to the fleet off Brest, himself keeping company with the Frenchmen. Being to leeward, and desirous of obtaining the weather-gage, as the safest situation for his own ship, he carried a heavy press of sail, and in the night of the 14th, having stretched on, as he thought, sufficiently for that purpose, put the *Loire* on the same tack as they were. About two a.m., it being then exceedingly dark, he found himself so near one of the largest ships as to hear the officer of the watch giving his orders. As the noise of putting about would have discovered the *Loire*'s situation, Captain Maitland very prudently abstained from doing so, until, by slacking the lee braces and luffing his ship to the wind, the enemy had drawn sufficiently ahead. At daylight he had the satisfaction to observe them four or five miles to leeward; and although he was chased both on that and the following day by a detachment from the enemy's squadron, he returned each evening and took his station on the French admiral's weather-beam, sufficiently near to keep sight of them till the morning. During the night between the 16th and 17th, several large ships were seen to windward running down, and which, on perceiving the *Loire* and those to leeward of her, made such signals as proved them also to be enemies. Captain Maitland had now no alternative but to make sail in order to get from between those two squadrons, the latter of which afterwards proved to be from Brest.

On 28 November 1806, Maitland was appointed to the *Emerald*, a 36-gun frigate. During the whole of her commission he cruised with ceaseless activity and made a very great number of captures. He was present with Lord Gambier's fleet outside Aix Roads in April 1809, when Cochrane made his famous fire-ship attack on the French fleet. The *Emerald* was one of the few ships which, on the 12th, were sent by Gambier, much against his will, to support Cochrane in the *Impérieuse*. One can well imagine that her gallant commander shared Cochrane's indignation at seeing so daring an enterprise shorn of its fruits by the weakness and irresolution of their chief.

Maitland's next appointment, dated 3 June 1813, was to the *Goliath*, a cut-down 74. He commanded her for twelve months on the Halifax and West

Captain Frederick Lewis Maitland,
(1777–1839).

India stations. Having been found seriously defective, she was paid off at Chatham in October 1814. In the following month Maitland was appointed to the *Boyne*, then fitting at Portsmouth for the flag of Sir Alexander Cochrane, commander-in-chief on the coast of America.

In January 1815 he was at Cork, and had collected a large fleet of transports and merchant vessels bound for America. The fleet was ready to sail, but was detained at Cove by a succession of strong westerly winds. Before the wind changed the news came that Napoleon had escaped from Elba.

Maitland's orders were at once countermanded, and he was removed to the ship with which his name will always be associated, the *Bellerophon*, 74. This famous old ship had fought on the First of June, at the Nile, and at Trafalgar; she was now once more to render a conspicuous service to the country.

She sailed from Plymouth with Sir Henry Hotham's squadron on 24 May 1815. Her commander's record of the memorable events which took place on board her during the following weeks is in the reader's hands, and nothing more need be said of them here. Let it suffice to note that the controversies which have raged around the story of Napoleon's exile, and which have tarnished so many reputations, have left Maitland's without a stain. "My reception in England," said Napoleon himself to Maitland, as he bade him farewell in the cabin of the *Bellerophon*, "has been very different from what I expected; but it gives me much satisfaction to assure you, that I feel your conduct to me throughout has been that of a gentleman and a man of honour."

Up to this point the materials for Maitland's biography are somewhat scanty. After this his journal, preserved at Lindores, gives us a very full record of his services.

In October 1818 he was appointed to the *Vengeur*, 74. She had been intended to bear the flag of Rear-Admiral Otway on the Leith station. In June 1819, however, she was ordered to join the squadron destined for South America under the command of Sir Thomas Hardy—Nelson's Hardy. The squadron left Spithead on 9 September, having on board Mr Thornton, HBM's minister to Brazil.

The following year was spent on the South American coast. In the disturbed political condition of the Continent, the duties of the British naval officers on the station were sometimes difficult and delicate, as British ships and British subjects frequently got into trouble with the forces of the revolted Spanish colonies. Maitland's time was spent chiefly at Rio de Janeiro. In 1807, when Napoleon's troops first appeared in the Tagus, the Portuguese Court had emigrated to Brazil and had been there ever since. Maitland's journal contains many amusing notes—not always printable—about King John VI and his disreputable family. "The king is very fond," he writes, "of comparing himself to the Regent of Great Britain, and does it as follows: 'His father is mad, so was my mother. I was Regent, so is he. I am very fat, so is he. I hate my wife, so does he.'" One anecdote which he tells of the king "must," he thinks, "raise him in the opinion of every British subject. When the Count de la Rocca was Spanish Ambassador at the Brazils, upon a rejoicing day the Portuguese ships were dressed with the national flag at the main, the British colours at the fore, and Spanish at the mizzen. The Count being at Court, drew the (then) Prince to a window which commanded a view of the harbour, and said to him, 'I have to ask your Royal Highness to look at those ships. The British colours are at the fore and my master's at the mizzen topmast-head. Were it only occasionally or alternately I should not complain, but it is never otherwise, and I feel it my duty, considering the close family connection that subsists between HM the King of Spain and your Royal Highness, to represent it to you, as it hurts my feelings in a manner I cannot express.' The King of Portugal tapped him gently on the shoulder and said to him, 'I'll tell you what, my friend, had it not been for that flag and the nation to whom it belongs, neither your master nor I would have had a flag to hoist at all.'"

That was true enough; still, the Portuguese were getting a little tired of the British flag. The Peninsular War had made Portugal almost a British dependency. Lord Beresford remained in command of the Portuguese army after the peace, and many other important appointments were held by English officers. The old monopoly of trade with Brazil had been broken down in favour of the English, to the ruin of not a few Portuguese merchants. These grievances, the continued absence of the Court in Brazil, and the general misgovernment of the country, had caused widespread discontent. Matters became critical after the outbreak of the Spanish revolution in January 1820.

In the spring of that year Beresford went out to Brazil to lay the state of affairs before the king, and to try to induce him to return to Portugal. The king would neither go himself nor allow his son to go. On August 13, Beresford sailed from Rio for Lisbon in Maitland's ship, the *Vengeur.*

While she was crossing the Atlantic, revolution broke out in Portugal. A military rising took place at Oporto on 24 August 1820, and when the *Vengeur* reached Lisbon on 10 October, Maitland found that the Regency had been deposed and a provisional Junta installed in the capital. Beresford was absolutely forbidden to land, even as a private individual, and was requested to leave the port without delay. The provisional Government told him plainly that in the existing state of public feeling they could not be responsible for his safety if he came on shore. After remaining for nearly a week on board the *Vengeur* in the Tagus, he went on to England in a packet-boat.

Maitland had expected to return to England, but at Lisbon he received orders to proceed immediately to the Mediterranean on secret service. On 27 October he reached the Bay of Naples, where he found a British squadron of five ships under Sir Graham Moore.

Serious political trouble had arisen in Naples. After the fall of Murat, Ferdinand IV had been restored to his throne by the Congress of Vienna, and in 1816 had assumed the title of King of the Two Sicilies. Under the restored monarchy discontent had been steadily growing. There had been no violent counter-revolution, but the interests of the country had been sacrificed without scruple to those of the king's friends, the swarm of courtiers who had shared his ignoble exile at Palermo. The revolutionary society of the Carbonari spread rapidly, alike in the army and in civil society. In Naples, as in Portugal, the Spanish revolution brought things to a crisis. On 2 July 1820, a military outbreak took place at Nola. This was followed by a general demand for a Constitution, which the king was powerless to resist. On 13 July 1820 he took the oath to the Constitution before the altar in the royal chapel.

A revolution in Naples would in all probability be followed by similar uprisings in the Papal States. Metternich was seriously alarmed. A conference of sovereigns and ministers to consider the affairs of Naples was arranged to be held at Troppau, in Moravia, in October 1820. England and France stood aloof from action, and the matter remained in the hands of the Emperor of Austria, the Czar, and the King of Prussia. It was resolved to invite King Ferdinand to meet his brother sovereigns at Laibach, in the Austrian province of Carniola, and through him to address a summons to the Neapolitans, requiring them, in the name of the three Powers and under threat of invasion, to abandon their Constitution.

Ferdinand could not leave the country without the consent of the Legislature. This was only given on his swearing to maintain the existing Constitution.

He did so with effusions of patriotism, and on 13 December he embarked on board the *Vengeur*, Maitland's ship, which conveyed him to Leghorn. On reaching Leghorn he addressed a letter to the sovereigns of the Great Powers repudiating all his recent acts. He reached Laibach in due course; and the Congress which took place there in January 1821 resulted in the restoration of absolutism at Naples and the occupation of the country by the Austrians.

It was a curious coincidence that Maitland should within a few years have had two sovereigns as passengers,—one the central figure of modern European history, the other the good-natured elderly buffoon who in this country is chiefly remembered as the husband of the friend of Lady Hamilton. Maitland thus records the voyage:—

Naples Bay, Wednesday, Dec. 13, 1820.—

A good deal of rain during the night; in the morning the wind to the east. A general order came on board for the captains to attend the admiral in their barges, for the purpose of attending the King of Naples off to the *Vengeur*, dressed in full uniform, with boots and pantaloons; a note, likewise, from the admiral telling me he intended to get the squadron under way and see the King out of the bay, the *Révolutionnaire* forming astern of the *Vengeur*, and he, with the five ships in line of battle, taking a position on our weather quarter; and when he takes his leave each ship is to pass under our stern, and there and then salute. The yards are to be manned and the ships to salute, beginning when the *Vengeur* fires her second gun. It is the intention of the French squadron to weigh also and stand out. At three p.m. the King of Naples came on board in Sir Graham Moore's barge, attended by the admiral and all the captains of the squadron except myself (as I stayed on board to receive him), and all the captains of the French squadron. He was saluted and cheered by all the ships except the Neapolitan, one of which manned her rigging, but no salute was given. As soon as the King was on board, unmoored, as did *Révolutionnaire* and *Duchesse de Berri*. Employed beating out. At about ten p.m. the *Révolutionnaire* was on our weather-bow when a thick heavy squall came on which blew the main topsail away. When the squall cleared away a little, I saw the *Révolutionnaire* close to us on our lee-bow, off the wind and stemming for us, and so near it was impossible the ships could clear each other. It therefore became necessary to adopt the measure which would soften the first blow as much as possible, and I ordered the helm to be put down. When the ship came head to wind she struck the *Révolutionnaire* just before the mainmast, slewed our cut-water right across, carried away the jib-boom, spritsail yard, &c., and then backed clear of her. A lad fell overboard from the *Révolutionnaire* and made a great noise, which enabled us to send a boat and pick him up, he having got upon one of our life-buoys. Got the runners up and the messenger through the hawse-holes, and set them up with the top tackles, which enabled us soon to make sail. Saw the *Duchesse de Berri* working out.

Dec. 14.—Strong breeze to the westward, with sea getting up. Saw *Révolutionnaire* to leeward. On examination, found the cut-water so much shook I determined to run on to Baia and secure the bowsprit; made signal to prepare to anchor, and bore up little after 8 a.m. Anchored in fifteen fathom water. The *Révolutionnaire* was examined also, when I found her mainmast was sprung; sent the master and carpenter to survey the damage she had sustained, two or three of her timbers being broke. They reported she might be put in a state to proceed in two days. Sent Lieutenant Drewry up to the Admiral with a letter giving an account of our disaster, and informing him I should proceed as soon as the weather would admit of it, taking *Révolutionnaire* with me if she was ready, otherwise directing him to follow. Got an answer from him in the evening offering the King any ship, even *Rochefort* (the flagship), if we could not proceed; and that he had ordered *Active* down here, to be ready to relieve *Révolutionnaire* if she could not go. In the morning, when the King came out, he took hold of both my hands, squeezed them, and shook them very heartily, saying, "I am infinitely obliged to you for the way in which you manoeuvred the ship last night, for had it not been for your promptitude she must have been dismasted." Dined with his Majesty, who sent me an invitation, and took my place, by his direction, at his right hand, in the way I used when Bonaparte was with me, and was a good deal struck with the similarity of situation. On the King's left sat the Princess of Paterna, created by him Duchess of Floridia. She is married to him, but does not assume the title of Queen, because she is not of blood royal. She is an uncommonly handsome woman for her time of life,—which the Prince of Babro tells me is very near fifty,—her manners pleasing, and quite those of a woman of high rank. He seems much attached to her, was particular in recommending good dishes to her, and once or twice when he spoke to her took her hand, and shook and prest it in a friendly affectionate way.

Baia, Dec. 15.—Strong gale, with very heavy squalls and showers of rain. The King is, in my opinion, much better at an anchor here than beating about the sea in a gale of wind. Employed securing the bowsprit. . . . Dined with the King, who told us several anecdotes of his sea excursions; and he really is a tolerably good sailor. In the evening a deputation of the Parliament came on board to condole with his Majesty on the accident that had befallen the ship, and to wish him a pleasant voyage and a speedy return to his country. In the evening pointed the yards to the wind. . . . While at dinner, HM sent out to have "Rule Britannia" played by the band, and drank success to the British Navy with three cheers.

Dec. 16.—In the morning the weather fine, with light wind W.S.W. Unmoored ship. . . . Stood over towards Capri till half-past one, when we tacked. The King told us at dinner he had been one of six who in seven days killed nine thousand quails on Capri Island, where in the month of May some years they come in millions. . . . Got round Ischia at 10 o'clock p.m.

Leghorn Roads, Wednesday, Dec. 20.—Employed all night beating into Leghorn Roads. . . . At eight, pratique boat came off and gave us pratique, and soon after the Governor of Leghorn came to pay his respects to the King, with a fine large barge. His Majesty soon got very impatient to go on shore, and would hardly give us time to make the necessary preparations for sending him out of the ship with due honours. At half-past nine he left the ship, accompanied by the Duchess of Floridia. . . . Saluted with twenty-one guns, and manned yards and cheered him as he left the ship. I accompanied him on shore, and when about to take my leave he asked me to dinner. I went, therefore, to the Grand Duke's palace, which is in the square; and when I got there the Marchese di Ruffo soon arrived, and, desiring my company in another room, produced the Order of St Ferdinand of the second class, and told me he had the King's sanction to present me with it; and when we were talking about it his Majesty came into the room and put it over my neck, and then led me by the hand and presented me to the Princess Paterna, when I returned my humble thanks to his Majesty, knelt, and kissed his hand. The princess told me it was her intention to send by me something as a present from her to my wife. The Marchese di Ruffo then came in and told me he had something further to communicate, and took me into the other room, when he gave me from his Majesty a remarkably handsome gold snuff-box with his portrait on it,—a very good likeness, set with twenty-four diamonds, some of them large, particularly four at the corners. He gave me also two other boxes, one for Captain Pellew and the other for the captain of the *Fleur de Lis*, and informed me he meant to give 3000 ducats to the *Vengeur's* ship's company and 1500 to each of the frigates. Dined with the King, and came off in the evening.

Dec. 21.— . . . To Franschetti the banker to obtain the money given by the King of Naples to the ships' companies; and after waiting a long time and having a great deal of trouble with a very stupid old fellow, we managed to get it from him. . . . Got my patent as Commander of the Order of St

Ferdinand and of Merit, for which I had to pay ten ducats as a fee to the secretary's clerk,—a part of the ceremony I did not bargain for, as the order cannot be of any use to me, there being a rule against officers accepting of foreign orders except in particular cases.

Dec. 22.— . . . At eleven the boats came off and brought all my traps, and a small parcel from the Princess Paterna, containing a very handsome gold necklace and bracelets, requesting I would accept them for her sake and present them to my wife. His Majesty, as well as the princess, have behaved to me in a most munificent way, having loaded me with favours and marks of their affection, which I shall ever remember with the warmest gratitude. As I have now done with the King of Naples, it may be as well to say a few words of his person and habits. He is a tall thin fair man, now seventy years of age, uncommonly robust and active for that time of life, which may be attributed in a great measure to his temperance and love of field-sports, which has been ever his ruling passion, and often occasioned him to neglect the more imposing and serious duties of a king. As a man, he must be liked by everyone who comes immediately in contact with him, as he is cheerful and good-humoured, though not a man of much information. While on board the ship he was generally up before daylight,—which at this season of the year is not saying much,—took a cup of coffee and a bit of biscuit,—to strengthen his stomach as he said,—and then said prayers, having two friars and a priest with him. At noon he dined, when he ate a very hearty meal, and drank about half a bottle of Neapolitan wine a good deal diluted with water, and ate nothing for the remainder of the day. In the evening he played picquet, and went to bed at eight or half past. . . .

The *Vengeur* returned to England in the spring of 1820, and Maitland was appointed to the *Genoa*, guardship at Portsmouth, from which he was superseded in October on the completion of his three years' continuous service on the peace establishment. The midshipmen of the *Genoa* presented him with a sword as a mark of respect.

Then followed a period of rest. In 1816 he had bought from his mother the estate of Lindores, near Newburgh, in Fifeshire, which had been in her family since 1569. Here he now spent several years, chiefly occupied in the improvement of the property. During the war he had made some £16,000 out of prize-money, part of which was spent in building the present mansion-house, overlooking the beautiful Loch of Lindores. In the spring of 1826 he visited London to arrange for the publication of the *Narrative*, which, after some fruitless negotiations with John Murray, was accepted by Colburn on satisfactory terms.

On 13 February 1827, Maitland was appointed to the *Wellesley*, 74. In December 1826, Mr Canning, in response to an appeal from the Portuguese Regency, had sent English troops to Lisbon to protect the Government of Portugal against the threatened attack of Spain. Maitland was ordered to Lisbon, and the *Wellesley* spent the autumn and winter of 1827 in the Tagus. After a spring cruise up the Mediterranean, she returned to England in May 1828. On 26 June she again sailed for the Mediterranean, carrying the flag of Admiral Sir Pulteney Malcolm, who was then going out to succeed Sir Edward Codrington in command of the Mediterranean station. On 24 August she joined the squadron under Codrington at Navarino.

Maitland remained in Greek waters for the next two years. The tragic drama of the Greek Revolution, after seven years of horrors, had now reached its final act. By the Treaty of London, in July 1827, England, Russia, and France had undertaken to put an end to the conflict in the East, and to establish the autonomy of Greece. In the following October the battle of Navarino had been fought, and the Turkish fleet destroyed. Ibrahim Pasha still held the fortresses of the Morea, which he was shortly to evacuate under the pressure of a French army corps. In April 1828 war had broken out between Turkey and Russia.

Desultory fighting was still going on in Crete, which had been utterly devastated by years of barbarous warfare. In October the *Wellesley* went to Suda Bay, and most of the winter was spent by Maitland on the coast of Crete, endeavouring to bring about an armistice, and superintending the blockade which the Powers had established in order to prevent military supplies from reaching the Turks in the island. The blockade was raised early in 1829; and during the following months Maitland visited nearly every point of interest on the Greek coast and in the Greek islands, as well as Sicily, the coast of Asia Minor, and Constantinople. Like most Englishmen who have served in the Levant, he developed a considerable respect for the Turk, and a quite unbounded contempt for the Greek. After the armistice negotiations in Crete he writes: "I found the conduct of the Turkish chiefs throughout manly, straightforward, and sincere, while that of their opponents was very much the reverse;" and in another place he writes of the Greeks that "a more perfidious, ferocious, and cruel race does not exist." Needless to say he did not think much of "our pretty Greek Committee."

In the summer of 1830 the *Wellesley* returned to England. Maitland attained his flag on 22 July 1830. At the reconstruction of the Order of the Bath in 1815 he had been made a CB; on 17 November 1830, he was advanced to be a KCB. In 1835 he received the Greek Order of the Redeemer.

During his South American and Mediterranean cruises Maitland kept a very full and interesting private journal. It reveals him to us as a man of immense mental activity and power of observation, hard humorous common sense, and an almost Pepysian interest in all the doings of mankind. Politics, archaeology, cricket, theatricals, scandal, the terms of a treaty, the menu of a good dinner, the armament of a foreign frigate, the toilette of a pretty woman, everything interests him, and is observed, remembered, and noted in his diary. A few extracts have been given; within the limits of this sketch they cannot be multiplied. His account of the slave-market at Constantinople may serve as a specimen of his power of picturesque description.

October 12, 1829.— . . . We then crossed the harbour, and went to the slave-market. It is held in a small square, with some houses in the middle, and on two sides of the square are small rooms, where the slaves for sale are kept until their turn comes to be put up. Adjoining the doors of these rooms or cells are raised platforms of wood on which a number of black women and girls were sitting; and I saw a few white ones inside. Outside these platforms are others, where the purchasers or those intending to purchase slaves were placed; and between the two platforms there is a passage three or four feet wide. At another corner of the market there were some black men and boys, chained by the legs to prevent their escaping, and among them we saw a very good-looking respectably dressed young man, also in chains. We were told he was a Georgian, but could not discover his history, though it is probable that his master had died, and that he was sold in consequence. He was smoking a pipe, and looked very disconsolate. A little after nine o'clock, the chief of the market arrived, and the sale began. Two or three black girls were first put up. A crier went round the square, followed by the slave for sale, passing through the passage before mentioned. When any person bids, the crier goes on, calling the sum bid, until someone bids higher, and continues calling till no more is bid, when the slave becomes the property of the highest bidder. There were three or four criers, with each a slave following them, going round the bazaar at the same time. At last a very pretty-looking white girl about sixteen years of age was put up for sale. Several bids had been made before I discovered her; and when I came up to the place where she was standing, Lambrino, the admiral's interpreter, asked the crier what sum was bid for her. He answered 1200 piastres; upon which the girl turned round in a rage, and said to Lambrino, "You dog-faced fellow, what is that to you?" and the interpreter being a little man, with high shoulders and a face very much shaped like a dog's, the girl's remark excited a general laugh. The crier, however, was by no means pleased at the young lady for making such a display of her temper, as it was likely to hurt her sale, and he therefore reprimanded her. They then passed on along the passage and came to one of the divans, where a man about forty was sitting smoking his pipe. He stopped the crier, and took the girl by the hand, felt all up her arm to the shoulder, then drew her a little nearer and opened her waistcoat, which exposed a beautiful white bosom, and the effect seemed electric, for he immediately bid 1300 piastres, and after pulling down the lower part of her veil so as to show the whole of her face, and looking at her teeth, he allowed the crier to proceed. The girl had been angry at Lambrino, and seemed a good deal distressed when the Turk was examining and handling her. I saw a blush of either modesty or indignation cross her countenance; but the instant the additional piastres were bid (whether from gratified vanity or what other cause I cannot say, for these poor creatures are very proud of bringing a high price) a smile of satisfaction beamed over her face, and she marched off in apparent good humour. I had seen enough of this horrid scene, and was tired of seeing a fellow-creature paraded about and handled like a horse, therefore was rejoiced when the admiral proposed we should leave it. Before we went away, a fellow, apparently an Armenian, came up and said he had a handsome young Greek girl for sale if we would like to see her. As, however, none of us under any circumstances could have purchased her, we declined his offer. . . .

A characteristic feature of Maitland's diary is his constant reference to his wife. He had married, in 1804, Catherine, second daughter of Daniel Connor of Ballybricken, County Cork. They had only one child, who died in infancy. Maitland loved his wife with lifelong devotion; wherever the service called him, her picture hung in his cabin, and he carried her image in his heart. Every letter she wrote to him is noted in his journal; and it is full of references to her in words of devoted attachment. Thus on the voyage home from South America in 1820 he writes: "Crossed the equator at eleven o'clock at night, and we are once more, Heaven be praised, in the northern hemisphere, which contains all I love and delight in in this world, and every mile we go draws us nearer to the sole mistress and possessor of my heart. . . . A more affectionate, kind, attached wife no man on earth is blessed with than myself." He was bitterly disappointed when from Lisbon he was ordered to the Mediterranean. As the ship passed Gibraltar he wrote: This was the day I had settled in my own mind that I was to arrive at Portsmouth, and there meet the dearest and best of wives. . . . I had expected this day to be the happiest of human beings, and now the event that would make me so appears as distant as ever." When he was at Naples, Mrs Maitland appears to have fallen under religious influences of the kind which often embitter family relations; and it is pathetic to read the expression of her husband's grief and anxiety lest the love which was the chief joy of his life should be estranged. "I fear much," he writes, "I shall have to regret the longest day I have to live, having left her in Scotland, instead of taking her abroad with me, as she was in a nest of fanatical foolish women

Lady Catherine Maitland. In April 1804 Frederick had married Catherine (d. 1865), second daughter of Daniel Connor of Ballybricken, Co. Cork; their only child died in infancy.

who have the madness to believe they are inspired from above." Happily the cloud soon passed, and he notes the receipt of "one of her own dear affectionate kind letters, such as she used formerly to write." A little later comes the joyful entry: "Bore up and made sail, with a fine strong Levant wind, which cleared us of the Gut of Gibraltar by noon; and I can now look forward with confidence to meeting my beloved Kate in about two weeks' time."

From 1832 to 1837 Maitland was Admiral Superintendent of the dockyard at Portsmouth. In July 1837 he was appointed commander-in-chief in the East Indies and China. He hoisted his flag on his own old ship the *Wellesley*, now commanded by Captain Thomas Maitland, afterwards Earl of Lauderdale, and sailed for Bombay on 11 October 1837. Lady Maitland accompanied him to the East.

When the advance from Bombay towards Afghanistan was made in 1838, it was decided that a naval force should proceed along the coast to co-operate with the troops. In January 1839, Maitland, in the *Wellesley*, joined the squadron in the Indus, and was requested by Sir John Keane, the military commander-in-chief, to "proceed to Kurrachee and take it." He arrived with his squadron before Kurrachee on 1 February 1839, and sent a flag of truce, summoning the fort of Manora, which formed the chief defence of the town. The Baluchi garrison refused all terms, and fired on the boats of the squadron, which were engaged in landing troops. The *Wellesley* accordingly opened fire, and soon reduced the fort to ruins and brought the commandant to terms. The British flag was hoisted on the fort by Lieutenant Jenkins of the *Wellesley*.

The town also surrendered, and was occupied by the 40th Regiment and the 2nd Bombay Native Infantry. The British Government thus easily obtained possession of the chief port of the Punjab.

After the capture of Kurrachee, Maitland returned to Bombay, and thence proceeded to Bushire, where difficulties had arisen with the Persian authorities. At an interview with the Governor, the Admiral demanded permission for himself and his officers to land and communicate freely with the British Resident. The Governor agreed to this, but refused to allow the Admiral to embark from the landing-place opposite the Residency. Next morning, 25 March, all the boats of the squadron, manned and armed, proceeded to the shore to protect the embarkation of the Admiral and other officers. The following account by an eye-witness of what then took place is given in Low's *History of the Indian Navy*:—

"The Persians had assembled to the number of several hundreds, and the Governor, with his body-guard, was determined to prevent, if possible, the property being shipped before the Residency. The first boat which approached the shore was fired upon, and one Persian had his musket presented at Captain Maitland. He was just on the eve of firing, when fortunately the Admiral and two Indian naval officers in a moment wrenched it from his hands, and kept possession of the piece, which they found loaded with a heavy charge. You may imagine how strongly inclined the marines must have been to fire. The benevolent spirit of the Admiral, however, would not allow it till the throwing of stones, and continued firing from the Persians, called forth two volleys, which caused the Persians to evacuate the breastwork. One was killed and two wounded; their fire upon us, fortunately, did not injure any one, but the Commodore and several other officers were struck with stones. After this the Residency was put in a state of defence, Captain Hennell (the Political Agent), had all the property conveyed as quickly as possible on board the *Wellesley*, *Elphinstone*, *Clive*, and *Emily*, and finally abandoned the Residency on the morning of the 28th, when surrounded by four or five hundred armed Persians, composed of Bushirees and Tungustanees, with Baukr Khan at their head. . . . And on the morning of the 29th the Wellesley and the other vessels reached Kharrack, bringing along with them the whole Residency establishment."

On 9 May 1839, the Officiating Secretary to the Government of India wrote to Maitland: "The Right Hon. the Governor-General highly applauds the cordial and able assistance offered by the officers and crews of HM's and the Hon. Company's ships, in the removal on board the ships of the Resident and his suite from the Residency at Bushire,—an operation which, but for their aid, might have been attended with difficulty and danger." Maitland was bitterly attacked by the Anglo-Indian press for his forbearance on this occasion, which it was said had lowered British prestige in the eyes of the

Persians. It is possible that our relations with Persia might have been improved by the slaughter of the Bushire mob by the *Wellesley*'s marines, but apparently the Admiral thought otherwise.

The Bushire incident was followed by a cruise round the Persian Gulf, in the course of which the Admiral had various interviews with the local chiefs, and impressed upon them the necessity of keeping the peace and respecting British interests.

It was his last service. He died at sea, off Bombay, on 30 November 1839. A letter from the late Admiral Philip Somerville, then a lieutenant on board the *Wellesley*, describes the closing scenes.

On our arrival at Bombay, Nov. 3," he writes, "the tents had not been pitched more than a week or so, and the one fitted by the Government for the Admiral was so very large that, after our arrival, he had to remain for some days on board ship ere it was ready. You may fancy the state the ground was in after five months' heavy rain,—the chill and damp scarcely possible to describe,—evaporation of course following the excessive heat of the day. A week had scarcely passed ere he felt its effects, but he could say nothing. On the 15th November I dined with him on shore. He seemed then tolerably well. On Sunday, 17th, he visited the ship, and returned to his tent. On the 18th he dined with her Majesty's 6th Regiment, and complained a little that day. The 21st, he was out to see our sailors and marines exercising. The complaint from that time made rapid progress. Saturday, 23rd, Lady Maitland went to a large party, but returned to the Admiral very early. Sunday 24th and Monday 25th he was dangerously ill; 26th and 27th, rather easier. Preparations were made for going to sea. On the 28th, the poor old fellow was brought off and hoisted on board in a palankeen. I saw him for a moment. Poor Sir Frederick lay with his head thrown back, his mouth a little open, his cheeks sunk, and his whole frame totally changed. He was conveyed to his cabin. We immediately got under way. All gloom, and solemn silence prevailed. I daresay some at least were in deep thought, some thinking of his former prosperity, others of the money he had made; perhaps some thought of the happy and honourable day on which Bonaparte surrendered. After lingering until Saturday the 30th, at 11.45 he expired. One can scarcely conceive the sensation caused by the mournful event. The countenances of all evinced deep sorrow for their chief, a man who was looked up to by all who knew him, and greatly beloved by those under his command. . . .

On Monday morning, preparations having been made the previous day, the troops of the garrison and boats from the ships began to assemble. The ship was painted black all over, and her yards topped in mourning. The body was conveyed in his own boat, the barge, the other boats following in order with their colours half-mast, presenting a very imposing sight. On leaving the ship, minute-guns began; and on the corpse reaching the shore, it was received with a guard of honour, and the fort commenced firing minute-guns as we formed in procession. The troops had their arms reversed, and the same people who received the Admiral that day fortnight at the dinner given by the 6th Regiment formed part of the parade that sorrowful moment. They lined the road through which we passed, and reached to the church. Here the body was received in the usual way, and all the respectable attendants followed it into the cathedral. The lesson was read by the officiating Archdeacon, and on coming to the grave in the aisle of the church, the Bishop read the service in a very affecting and solemn manner. After the ceremony we returned to our respective ships.

A monument to Sir Frederick's memory was erected in Bombay Cathedral by the officers of his command. "Among names," writes Lieutenant Low in his History, "which will ever be held in affection by the officers whose record of service is now 'as a tale that is told,' that of Maitland, the gallant and chivalrous seaman, to whom the mighty Napoleon surrendered his sword on the quarter-deck of the *Bellerophon*, will ever be prominent; and this record of his worth and nobility of character, and that other memorial on the walls of the Cathedral Church of St Thomas, will testify to the grateful remembrance in which his memory is held by the officers of the Indian Navy."

Napoleon and his defeated army head westwards towards Paris after the Battle of Waterloo, 19–20 June 1815. The battle had commenced at midday on Sunday 18 June 1815. Napoleon finally retreated from his headquarters at *La Belle Alliance* during the later part of the evening on the 18th accompanied by the remains of the Old Guard.

2

The Surrender of Napoleon

On Wednesday the 24th of May, 1815, I sailed from Cawsand Bay, in command of His Majesty's ship *Bellerophon*, and under the orders of Rear-Admiral Sir Henry Hotham, whose flag was hoisted in the *Superb*. I received sealed instructions, part of which were to be opened on getting to sea, and part only to be examined in the event of my being separated from the Admiral. Those which I opened contained directions to detain, and send into port, all armed vessels belonging to the Government of France

On Sunday the 28th of May, we joined His Majesty's ships *Astrea* and *Telegraph*, stationed off Isle Dieu, on a secret service; and the following day, three transports, under charge of the *Helicon*, arrived from England, having on board arms and ammunition, to supply the Royalists in La Vendée, for whose support and assistance I now found the squadron, of which the *Bellerophon* formed one, was destined.

On Tuesday the 30th of May, I received orders from Sir Henry Hotham, to take the *Eridanus* under my command, and proceed off Rochefort, for the purpose of preventing a corvette from putting to sea, which, according to information received by the British Government, was to carry proposals from Bonaparte to the West India Colonies, to declare in his favour. I had likewise orders to reconnoitre the Roadstead of Rochefort, and report to the Admiral the number and state of the ships of war lying there. Accordingly, on the 31st of May, I ran into Basque Roads, and found at anchor, under Isle d'Aix, two large frigates, a ship corvette, and a large brig, all ready for sea, which I afterwards ascertained to be the *Méduse*, *Saale*, *Balladière*, and *Epervier*. Nothing occurred worth mentioning until the 9th of June, when the *Vésuve* French corvette came in from the northward, and got into Rochefort, notwithstanding every effort to prevent her; the ships under my orders having been driven to the southward, during the night, by a strong northerly wind, accompanied by a southerly current. She was from Guadaloupe, and immediately on passing the Chasseron light-house, hoisted the tricoloured flag.

On the 18th of June, I detained and sent to Sir Henry Hotham, the *Æneas* French store-ship, commanded by a lieutenant of the navy, with a crew of fifty men, loaded with ship-timber for the arsenal of Rochefort; but he, being of opinion that she did not come within the intention of the order, liberated her.

On the 21st of June, I detained and sent to the Admiral, under charge of the *Eridanus*, the *Marianne* French transport, from Martinique, having on board 220 of the 9th regiment of light infantry, coming to France to join the army under Bonaparte. The *Eridanus* was sent to England with her, and did not return to me, being employed on other service.

On the 27th of June, the *Cephalus* joined us, bringing with her the declaration of war against France; after which we were employed several days, taking and destroying chasse-marées, and other small coasting vessels.

On the 28th of June, I received intelligence, from one of the vessels captured, of Napoleon's defeat at Waterloo; and on the 30th, a boat came off from Bordeaux, bringing the following letter, without date or subscription, written on very thin paper in English, and concealed within a quill. I give the contents verbatim.

Copy of a Letter received by Captain Maitland, of HMS *Bellerophon*, off Rochefort, on the 30th of June, 1815, without date or subscription:

With great degree of certainty, being informed that Bonaparte might have come last night through this city from Paris, with the new Mayor of Bordeaux, with a view to flight, by the mouth of this river, or La Teste, the author of the last note sent by Mr ———— hastily drops these few lines, to give the British Admiral advice of such intention, that he may instantly take the necessary steps, in order to seize the man. His ideas will certainly have brought him to think it natural, that the British stations will be less upon their guard in this quarter than any where else. The writer benefits by this opportunity to inform the Admiral that, since the last note, some alteration has taken place with regard to the troops spread in these two Divisions; in lieu of 800 to 1000 in this city, there are now 5000, which is supposed owing to the intention of compressing the minds of this populace in this decisive instant.

It is supposed the British Admiral is already informed of the Grand Army being totally defeated and destroyed, the abdication of Bonaparte, &c. and the arrival of the allies near the Capital.

An attempt should be made on this Coast, with no less than 8000 men altogether. Immediate steps are wanted to put a stop to the supposed flight.

Should the attempt be made on the Coast from La Teste to Bordeaux,

Chart of Basque Roads

an immediate diversion should be made on this side; the success is beyond any doubt.

A sharp eye must be kept on all American vessels, and particularly on the *Susquehannah*, of Philadelphia, Captain Caleb Cushing; General Bertand and another goes with him. The two entrances of Bordeaux and La Teste must be kept close; a line or two is expected, on the return of the bearer from the Admiral, or Chief Officer on the Station. As this is writing, the news is spread generally, that the Duc de Berri and Lord Wellington are in Paris.

The note alluded to had been received, and forwarded unopened, to the Admiral in Quiberon Bay.

Though my attention was called so strongly to Bordeaux, or la Teste d'Arcasson, as the parts of the coast from whence Bonaparte would probably attempt to escape, it was my decided opinion that Rochefort was much more likely to be the port where the trial would be made. I therefore sent the *Myrmidon* off Bordeaux, the *Cephalus* to Arcasson, and remained with only the *Bellerophon*, off Rochefort. From this period, until my return to England, the ship was never, by day or night, more than three miles from the land. Considering it of much importance to communicate the intelligence contained in the letter from Bordeaux, to my commanding officer, with as little delay as possible; as I had no vessel left with me, after detaching the two ships under my orders, I sent the *Bellerophon*'s barge, under the charge of a lieutenant, with directions to endeavour to join some one of the cruisers stationed off Isle Dieu. I gave him an order, addressed to the Captain of any of His Majesty's ships he might fall in with, to proceed without loss of time, to join the Admiral in Quiberon Bay, with the despatch accompanying it.

This boat was fortunate enough to fall in with His Majesty's ship *Cyrus*, Captain Carrol; who, in consequence, after hoisting in the barge, proceeded to Quiberon Bay.

As the coasting-vessels were not worth sending into port for condemnation, (and considering the circumstances under which the ship I commanded was placed, I should not have felt justified in weakening her complement, even for a prize of value,) I was in the habit of using such captures, as marks for the men to practice firing at. The *Cephalus* had a chasse-marée in tow for that purpose,— when the letter, inserted above, was received; and I detached her so shortly afterwards, that Captain Furneaux had no opportunity of destroying her, but was obliged to cast her off. After he had left me some time, I observed the vessel drifting to sea, and determined to run down and sink her. While approaching her in this view. I was sweeping the horizon with my glass, when I discovered, at a considerable distance, a small white speck on the water, which had the appearance of a child's boat with paper sails; but I could plainly perceive something that had motion in it; and, after firing on and destroying the chasse marée, I stood towards the object which had engaged my attention, and found it to be a small punt, about eight feet long, flatbottomed, and shaped more like a butcher's tray than a boat. In it were a young man about eighteen years of age, and a boy about twelve, who had got into the punt to amuse themselves, and, happening to lose one of their oars, were drifted to sea. They had been thirty-six hours without refreshment of any kind, and with only one oar and a bit of board, which they had formed into something like another; they were quite exhausted with fatigue, and their hands very much blistered. When we picked them up, there was a strong breeze blowing off the land, so that there cannot be a doubt, had not Providence sent us to their assistance, they must have perished. I kept the boys on board two or three days, for the purpose of recruiting their strength, and then landed them with the punt, close to their village, to the great joy and wonder of their parents and countrymen.

On the first of July, we spoke a ship from Rochefort, the master of which gave information, that the frigates in Aix Roads had taken in their powder, and were in all respects ready to put to sea; also, that several gentlemen in plain clothes, and some ladies, supposed to form part of Bonaparte's suite, had arrived at Isle d'Aix: in short, upon the whole, that there was little doubt of its being his intention to effect his escape, if possible, from that place, in the frigates. On receiving this information, I anchored the *Bellerophon* as close to the French squadron as the batteries would permit, kept guard-boats rowing all night, and prepared my ship's company for the description of action in which I thought it was probable they would be engaged. I trained one hundred of the stoutest men, selecting them from the different stations in the ship; it being my intention, after firing into and silencing one frigate, to run the *Bellerophon* alongside of her, throw that party in, and then, leaving her in charge of the first lieutenant, to have proceeded in chase of the other.

His Majesty's ship *Phoebe* joined us this evening, and brought with her the *Bellerophon*'s barge. Captain Hillyar having orders to take a station off Bordeaux, I recalled the *Myrmidon* from that service.

On the 7th of July, I received a letter from Sir Henry Hotham, together with fresh orders, from which the following are extracts:–

Extract of a Letter from Rear-Admiral Sir Henry Hotham, KCB, addressed to Captain Maitland of HMS *Bellerophon*, dated Quiberon Bay, July 6, 1815.

It is impossible to tell which information respecting Bonaparte's flight may be correct; but, in the uncertainty, it is right to attach a certain degree of credit to all: that which I now act on, is received this morning, from the chief of the Royalists, between the Loire and the Vilaine.

Although the force of the *Bellerophon* would be sufficient for the ships at Isle d'Aix, if they were to give you an opportunity of bringing them to action together, you cannot stop them both, if the frigates separate; I am, therefore, now anxious you should have a frigate with you: therefore if any of them should be with you, keep her for the time I have specified; but if you have no frigate, and this should be brought to you by a twenty-gun ship, keep her with you for the same time; she will do to keep sight of a French frigate, although she could not stop her.

If this is delivered to you by Lord John Hay of the *Opossum*, do not detain him, as her force would be of no use to you, and I want him particularly, to examine vessels which sail from the Loire.

Extract of an Order from Rear-Admiral Sir Henry Hotham, KCB.; addressed to Captain Maitland of HMS *Bellerophon* dated *Superb*, Quiberon Bay, 6 July 1815.

Having this morning received information that it is believed Napoleon Bonaparte has taken his road from Paris for Rochefort, to embark from thence for the United States of America, I have to direct you will use your best endeavours to prevent him from making his escape in either of the frigates at Isle d'Aix; for which purpose you are, notwithstanding former orders, to keep any frigate which may be with you, at the time you receive this letter, in company with the ship you command, for the space of ten days, to enable you to intercept them in case they should put to sea together: but if you should have no frigate with you at the above time, you will keep the ship delivering this, (which will probably be the *Slaney* or *Cyrus*,) in company with the *Bellerophon*, ten days, and then allow her to proceed in execution of the orders her Captain has received from me.

The *Slaney* brought the letter and order, parts of which are extracted above, and having no frigate in company, I detained her as part of the force under my command, though she was, on the 8th, sent down to the Mamusson passage, with orders for Captain Green of the *Daphne*, and did not return until the evening of the 11th.

On the 8th of July, I was joined by a chasse-marée bringing a letter from Sir Henry Hotham, part of which is as follows:–

Extract of a Letter from Rear-Admiral Sir Henry Hotham, KCB, addressed to Captain Maitland, of HMS *Bellerophon*, dated *Superb*, Quiberon Bay, July 7, 1815.

Having sent every ship and vessel out from this bay, to endeavour to intercept Bonaparte, I am obliged to send the chasse marée, which has been employed in my communications with the Royalists, with this letter, to acquaint you that the *Ferret* brought me information last evening, after the *Opossum* had left me, from Lord Keith, that Government received, on the night of the 30th, an application from the rulers of France, for a passport and safe conduct for Bonaparte to America, which had been answered in the negative, and, therefore, directing an increase of vigilance to intercept him: but it remains quite uncertain where he will embark; and, although it would appear by the measures adopted at home, that it is expected he will sail from one of the northern ports, I am of opinion he will go from one of the southern places, and I think the information I sent you yesterday by the *Opossum* is very likely to be correct; namely, that he had taken the road to Rochefort; and that he will probably embark in the frigates at Isle d'Aix; for which reason I am very anxious you should have force enough to stop them both, as the *Bellerophon* could only take one, if they separated, and that might not be the one he would be on board of. I have no frigate to send you; if one should join me in time, I will send her to you, and I hope you will have two twenty-gun ships with you. I imagine, from what you said in your letter by your barge, that you would not have kept the *Endymion* with you, especially as the *Myrmidon* would have rejoined you, by the arrangements I sent down by the *Phoebe* for Sir John Sinclair to take her place off the Mamusson; there-fore, I trust that my last order to Captain Hope will not have deprived you of his assistance, but hope it may have put him in a better situation than before. The *Liffey* is seventy or eighty miles west from Bordeaux, and the *Pactolus*, after landing some person in the Gironde, goes off Cape Finisterre, where the *Swiftsure* is also gone; and many ships are looking out in the Channel and about the latitude of Ushant.

Bonaparte is certainly not yet gone; I presume he would naturally await the answer from our Government, which only left London on the 1st; my own opinion is, that he will either go with a force that will afford him some kind of security, or in a merchant vessel to avoid suspicion.

The orders from the Admiralty, received last evening, are, that the ships which are looking out for him, should remain on that service till further orders, or till they know he is taken, and not regard the time of ten days or a fortnight, which they first named: therefore you will govern yourself by that, and keep any ship you have with you till one of those events occurs, without attending to the ten days I specified in my letter to you by the *Opossum* yesterday, and make the same known to any ship you may communicate with. The information you sent me, which had been transmitted to you from Bordeaux, is now proved to have been erroneous, by our knowing that Bonaparte was at Paris as late as the 30th of June, and that paper must have been written on the 29th, as you received it on the 30th. The *Eridanus* will not rejoin you; she has been stationed, by Lord Keith, off Brest.

Let me know by the return of the chasse-marée, particularly, what ships you have with you, and where the other ships are, as far as you know, and what position you keep in. If you had ships enough to guard Basque Roads, and the Channel between Isle d'Oleron and the long sand (where a frigate may pass), you would be sure of keeping them in, by anchoring; but that would afford you little chance of taking Bonaparte, which is the thing to be desired; therefore I think you would be better off the light-house, where I dare say you keep yourself; and on that particular subject I do not think it necessary to give you any instructions, as I depend on your using the best means that can be adopted to intercept the fugitive; on whose captivity the repose of Europe appears to depend. If he should be taken, he is to be brought to me in this bay, as I have orders for his disposal; he is to be removed from the ship in which he may be found, to one of his Majesty's ships.

Nothing of consequence occurred on the 9th; but on the 10th of July, at daylight, the officer of the watch informed me that a small schooner was standing out from the French squadron towards the ship: upon which I ordered everything to be ready for making sail in chase, supposing she might be sent for the purpose of reconnoitring. On approaching, she hoisted a flag of truce, and joined us at seven a.m. She proved to be the *Mouche*, tender to the ships of war at Isle d'Aix, and had on board, General Savary Duc de Rovigo, and Count Las Cases, chamberlain to Bonaparte, charged with a letter from Count Bertrand (Grand Marechal de Palais) addressed to the Admiral commanding the British Cruisers before the port of Rochefort.

Soon after the *Mouche* arrived, I was joined by the *Falmouth*, bringing me a letter and secret orders from Sir Henry Hotham, some extracts from which I shall insert for the better understanding what follows, previous to entering into what passed with Bonaparte's attendants.

Extract of a Letter from Rear-Admiral Sir Henry Hotham, KCB, addressed to Captain Maitland, of HMS *Bellerophon*; not dated, but must have been written on the 8th of July, 1816.

> I sent a chasse-marée to you yesterday with a letter, and you will now receive by the *Falmouth*, officially, the orders which I therein made you acquainted with.
>
> I send you four late and very interesting French papers, by which you will see all that has been done and said on the subject of providing for Bonaparte's escape from France: you will see that the Minister of the Marine had been directed to prepare ships of war for that purpose; that they were placed at Bonaparte's disposal; and that two frigates in particular had been provided for him: also that it was announced to the two Chambers, that he left Paris at four o'clock on the 29th; likewise that it was believed in Paris, he had taken the road by Orleans to Rochefort; and I have no doubt that the two frigates at Isle d'Aix are intended for him, and I hope you will think so too, and I am sure you will use your utmost endeavours to intercept him. I am sorry I have not a frigate to send you; I have literally none but the *Endymion* under my orders. Captain Paterson is off Brest, by Lord Keith's order; and the *Phoebe* is also ordered to that station, when the *Hebrus* arrives off the Gironde.
>
> The attention at home appears to be paid chiefly to the ports in the Channel, but I have received no additional means whatever to guard those of the Bay. I have long been expecting a frigate from the Irish station, but none has yet appeared; and I have written to Lord Keith for two frigates; but they cannot join me in time, I fear.

Extract of an Order from Rear-Admiral Sir Henry Hotham, KCB., addressed to Captain Maitland, of HMS *Bellerophon*, dated HMS *Superb*, Quiberon Bay, 8th July, 1815.

The Lords Commissioners of the Admiralty having every reason to believe that Napoleon Bonaparte meditates his escape, with his family, from France to America, you are hereby required and directed, in pursuance of orders from their Lordships, signified to me by Admiral the Right Honourable Viscount Keith, to keep the most vigilant look-out for the purpose of intercepting him; and to make the strictest search of any vessel you may fall in with; and if you should be so fortunate as to intercept him, you are to transfer him and his family to the ship you command, and there keeping him in careful custody, return to the nearest port in England (going into Torbay in preference to Plymouth) with all possible expedition; and on your arrival you are not to permit any communication whatever with the shore, except as herein after directed; and you will be held responsible for keeping the whole transaction a profound secret, until you receive their Lordships' further orders.

In case you should arrive at a port where there is a flag-officer, you are to send to acquaint him with the circumstances, strictly charging the officer sent on shore with your letter, not to divulge its contents: and if there should be no flag-officer at the port where you arrive, you are to send one letter express to the Secretary of the Admiralty, and another to Admiral Lord Keith, with strict injunctions of secrecy to each officer who may be the bearer of them.

Messrs Savary and Las Cases, who came on board, from the Schooner above mentioned, at seven o'clock on the 10th of July, presented the following letter to me:

Le 9 Juillet, 1815.

Monsieur l'Amiral,

L'Empereur Napoléon ayant abdiqué le pouvoir, et choisi les États Unis d'Amérique pour s'y refugier, s'est embarqué sur les deux frégates qui sont dans cette rade, pour se rendre à sa destination. Il attend le sauf conduit du Gouvernement Anglais, qu'on lui a annoncé, et qui me porte à expédier le présent parlementaire, pour vous demander, Mons. l'Amiral, si vous avez connoissance du dit sauf conduit; ou si vous pensez qu'il soit dans l'intention du Gouvernement Anglais de se mettre de l'empêchement à notre voyage aux l'États Unis. Je vous serai extrêmement obligé de me donner la-dessus les renseignemens que vous pouvez avoir.

Je charge les porteurs de la présente lettre de vous faire agréer mes remercîmens et mes excuses, pour la peine qu'elle a pu vous donner.

J'ai l'honneur d'être,

    Monsieur l'Amiral, de Votre Excellence, &c. &c.

    Le Grand Maréchal Cte. BERTRAND

À Monsieur l'Amiral commandant
les Croisières avant Rochefort.

Translation

Sir,

The Emperor Napoleon having abdicated the throne of France, and chosen
the United States of America as a retreat, is, with his suite, at present
embarked on board the two frigates which are in this port, for the purpose of
proceeding to his destination. He expects a passport from the British Government, which has been promised to him, and which induces me to send the
present flag of truce, to demand of you, Sir, if you have any knowledge of the
above-mentioned passport, or if you think it is the intention of the British
Government to throw any impediment in the way of our voyage to the
United States. I shall feel much obliged by your giving me any information
you may possess on the subject.

I have directed the bearers of this letter to present to you my thanks, and
to apologise for the trouble it may cause.

I have the honour to be,
Your Excellency's most obedient, &c. &c.
Grand Marshal Count BERTRAND.

To the Admiral commanding the
Squadron before Rochefort.

The bearers of the letter had instructions to demand of me, whether I would
prevent Bonaparte from proceeding in a neutral vessel, provided I could not
permit the frigates to pass with him on board. Having received, in my orders,
the strictest injunctions to secrecy, and feeling that the force on the coast, at
my disposal, was insufficient to guard the different ports and passages from
which an escape might be effected, particularly should the plan be adopted
of putting to sea in a small vessel; I wrote the following reply to the above
communication; hoping, by that means, to induce Napoleon to remain for the
Admiral's answer, which would give time for the arrival of reinforcements.

HMS Bellerophon
off Rochefort, July 10th, 1815.

Sir,

I have to acknowledge the receipt of your letter of yesterday's date,
addressed to the Admiral commanding the English cruisers before Rochefort,

An engraving of Emanuel Auguste Dieudonné Marius Joseph Marquis Las Cases, (1776-1842). Las Cases was arrested on 25 November 1816 by Sir Hudson Lowe and deported on 30 December 1816 together with his son.

acquainting me that the Emperor, having abdicated the throne of France, and chosen the United States of America as an asylum, is now embarked on board the frigates, to proceed for that destination, and awaits a passport from the English Government; and requesting to know if I have any knowledge of such passport; or if I think it is the intention of the English Government to prevent the Emperor's voyage.

In reply, I have to acquaint you, that I cannot say what the intentions of my Government may be; but, the two countries being at present in a state of war, it is impossible for me to permit any ship of war to put to sea from the port of Rochefort.

As to the proposal made by the Duc de Rovigo and Count Las Cases, of allowing the Emperor to proceed in a merchant vessel; it is out of my power,—without the sanction of my commanding officer, Sir Henry Hotham, who is at present in Quiberon Bay, and to whom I have forwarded your despatch,—to allow any vessel, under whatever flag she may be, to pass with a personage of such consequence.

I have the honour to be, Sir,
        Your very humble servant,
            Fred. L. Maitland,
                Captain of HMS Bellerophon.

Le Grand Maréchal
Comte Bertrand.

The Duke of Rovigo and Count Las Cases remained on board between two and three hours, during which time I had a great deal of conversation with them, on the state of affairs in France; in which they did all they could to impress me with the idea that Bonaparte was not reduced to the necessity of quitting Europe; but that, in doing so, he was actuated solely by motives of humanity; being unwilling, they said, that any further effusion of blood should take place on his account. They declared also, that his party was still very formidable in the centre and south of France, and that, if he chose to protract the war, he might still give a great deal of trouble; and that, although his ultimate success might not be probable, there was still a possibility of fortune turning in his favour, and therefore they argued it was the interest of England to allow him to proceed to America. To all this I could give little or no reply, being quite ignorant of what had occurred in France, further than the decisive victory obtained by the Duke of Wellington at Waterloo. During the time the Frenchmen were with me, I received some French newspapers from Sir Henry Hotham; but my time was so fully occupied in writing to him, and in discussions with my visitors, that it was not in my power to read them: I therefore drew them back to the subject that had occasioned their visit, and said, "Supposing the British Government should be induced to grant a passport for Bonaparte's going to America, what pledge could he give that he would not return, and put England, as well as all Europe, to the same expense of blood and treasure that has just been incurred?"

General Savary made the following reply:

When the Emperor first abdicated the throne of France, his removal was brought about by a faction, at the head of which was Talleyrand, and the sense of the nation was not consulted: but in the present instance he has voluntarily resigned the power. The influence he once had over the French people is past; a very considerable change has taken place in their sentiments towards him, since he went to Elba; and he could never regain the power he had over their minds: therefore he would prefer retiring into obscurity, where he might end his days in peace and tranquillity; and were he solicited to ascend the throne again, he would decline it.

"If that is the case," I said, "why not ask an asylum in England?"

He answered:

There are many reasons for his not wishing to reside in England: the climate is too damp and cold; it is too near France; he would be, as it were, in the centre of every change and revolution that might take place there, and would be subject to suspicion; he has been accustomed to consider the English as his most inveterate enemies, and they have been induced to look upon him as a monster, without one of the virtues of a human being.

This conversation took place while I was writing my despatches to Sir Henry Hotham; and the Frenchmen were walking in the cabin, frequently interrupting me, to enforce their statement of Bonaparte's situation being by no means so desperate as might be supposed; from which I took the liberty of drawing a conclusion directly opposite to the one they were desirous of impressing on my mind.

Captain Knight, of the *Falmouth*, who carried my despatches to the Admiral, was present during the whole of this conversation, but did not join in it. This was the first certain information I had received of Bonaparte's position since the battle of Waterloo.

Tuesday, the 11th.—About noon, a small boat came off from the Island of Oleron, to where the ship was at anchor in Basque Roads, rowed by four men, in which sat two respectable-looking countrymen, who asked for the Captain; and upon my being pointed out to them, requested to speak with me in private. When shown into the cabin, where I went accompanied by Captain Gambier, of the *Myrmidon*, they acquainted me, that a message had been sent from Isle d'Aix, early that morning, for a man who was considered the best pilot on the island for the Mamusson passage, being the only person that had ever taken a frigate through; that a large sum of money had been offered to him to pilot a vessel to sea from that passage, and that it certainly was Bonaparte's intention to escape from thence; either in the corvette, which had moved down some days before, or in a Danish brig, which was then lying at anchor near the entrance.

On receiving this information, I immediately got under weigh, and though the flood-tide had just made in, beat the ships out of the Pertuis d'Antioche before it was dark, when I sent the *Myrmidon* off the Mamusson, with orders to anchor close in with the entrance, when the weather would admit of it; while I remained with the *Bellerophon* and *Slaney*, which rejoined me that evening, under weigh between the light-houses.

On the 12th of July, the *Cyrus* being seen in the offing, I ordered her by telegraph to take a position close in with the Baleine light-house, and to examine strictly every vessel that might attempt to put to sea from the Pertuis de Breton, as Bonaparte was on the spot, endeavouring to escape to America.

The same evening, the white flag made its appearance for the first time on the towers of Rochelle; on seeing which, I felt it my duty to run into Basque Roads, accompanied by the *Slaney*; and having anchored, I hoisted the

Bourbon colours at the main-top-gallant mast-head, and fired a royal salute. During the whole of this afternoon, however, two tricoloured flags were kept flying in Rochelle; and before sunset all the white flags were struck, and everywhere replaced by those of Bonaparte.

On the 13th of July, nothing of importance occurred, except the white flag being once more hoisted all over Rochelle, as well as on the Isle of Oleron, to the entire exclusion of the tricoloured ensign. We could plainly perceive, that the frigates, from whom we were distant about three miles, were perfectly ready to put to sea, should an opportunity offer; having their sterns covered with vegetables, their top-gallant yards across, studding sail gear rove, and numerous boats passing between them and the island the whole day:– all indications, well known to professional men, of preparing for sea.

The ships under my command were accordingly kept with slip buoys on their cables, and, as soon as it was dark, the top-sail and top-gallant yards were swayed to the mast-heads, the sails stopt with rope yarns, and everything kept ready to make sail at a moment's warning. Guardboats were also kept rowing all night, as near the frigates as they could venture, having signals established to show in the event of the enemy getting under sail.

On the 14th of July, at daybreak, the officer of the watch informed me, that the *Mouche* was standing out from Isle d'Aix, bearing a flag of truce, which I ordered to be accepted. Here it is necessary to mention, that the British flag of truce, being a white flag at the fore-top-gallant mast-head, which was also hoisted as a matter of course when Bonaparte was received on board, has by some persons been construed into the Bourbon flag, and thence into an intentional insult to him. It never was my intention, nor do I believe it could have been that of any British officer, to treat with insult any fallen enemy, much less one who had shown such confidence as to throw himself on the protection of his former foe.

When the schooner, the *Mouche*, reached the ship, Count Las Cases came on board, attended by General Count Lallemand. This meeting was highly interesting to me, as Lallemand had been a prisoner for three weeks in the *Camelion* under my command in Egypt, with Junot, whose Aide-de-Camp he then was; and General Savary, who accompanied Count Las Cases in his first visit to the *Bellerophon*, had lived nearly as long at Sir Sydney Smith's table with me, at the Turkish camp at El Arish, when the convention, which takes its name from that place, was under discussion, being Aide-de-Camp to General Dessaix, who negotiated on the part of the French.

On their coming on board, I made the signal for the Captain of the *Slaney*, being desirous of having a witness to any conversation that might pass, as our communications were chiefly verbal: he arrived while we were at breakfast.

When Count Las Cases came on the quarter-deck, he informed me that he was sent off to learn whether I had received an answer from the Admiral to the letter he had brought off on the 10th instant. I told him that I had not, but, in consequence of the despatch which I had forwarded to him, I had not a doubt he would immediately repair here in person, and I was hourly in expectation of seeing him, adding, "If that was the only reason you had for sending off a flag of truce, it was quite unnecessary, as I informed you, when last here, that the Admiral's answer, when it arrived, should be forwarded to the frigates by one of the *Bellerophon*'s boats; and I do not approve of frequent communications with an enemy by means of flags of truce." I then went into the cabin and ordered breakfast, to prevent further discussion until the arrival of Captain Sartorius.

When breakfast was over, we retired to the after-cabin. Count Las Cases then said:

> The Emperor is so anxious to spare the further effusion of human blood, that he will proceed to America in any way the British Government chooses to sanction, either in a French ship of war, a vessel armed *en flute*, a merchant vessel, or even in a British ship of war.

To this I answered:

> I have no authority to agree to any arrangement of that sort, nor do I believe my Government would consent to it; but I think I may venture to receive him into this ship, and convey him to England: if, however, [I added], he adopts that plan, I cannot enter into any promise, as to the reception he may meet with, as, even in the case I have mentioned, I shall be acting on my own responsibility, and cannot be sure that it would meet with the approbation of the British Government.

There was a great deal of conversation on this subject, in the course of which Lucien Bonaparte's name was mentioned, and the manner in which he had lived in England alluded to; but I invariably assured Las Cases most explicitly, that I had no authority to make conditions of any sort, as to Napoleon's reception in England. In fact, I could not have done otherwise, since, with the exception of the order I had received, I had no instructions for my guidance, and was, of course, in total ignorance of the intention of His Majesty's ministers as to his future disposal. One of the last observations Las Cases made before quitting the ship was, "Under all circumstances, I have little doubt that you will see the Emperor on board the *Bellerophon*;" and, in fact, Bonaparte must have determined on that step before Las Cases came on board, as his letter to his Royal Highness the Prince Regent is dated the 13th of July, the day before this conversation.

During the above-mentioned conversation, I asked Las Cases where Bonaparte then was? He replied, "At Rochefort; I left him there yesterday evening." General Lallemand then said, "The Emperor lives at the Hotel in the Grand Place, and is now so popular there, that the inhabitants assemble every evening in front of the house, for the purpose of seeing him, and crying, 'Vive l'Empereur!'"

I then asked how long it would take to go there: Las Cases answered, "As the tide will be against us, it will require five or six hours." Why these false statements were made, I cannot pretend to say; but it is very certain that Bonaparte never quitted the frigates or Isle d'Aix, after his arrival there on the 3rd of July.

General Lallemand took occasion to ask me if I thought there would be any risk of the people, who might accompany Bonaparte, being given up to the Government of France: I replied, "Certainly not; the British Government never could think of doing so, under the circumstances contemplated in the present arrangement."

They left me about half-past nine a.m. In the course of the day, I was joined by the *Myrmidon*, Captain Gambier, who had been sent to me by Captain Green, of the *Daphne*, with a letter he had received from Captain Aylmer, of the *Pactolus*, in the Gironde, bringing information that it was the intention of Bonaparte to escape from Rochefort in a Danish sloop, concealed in a cask stowed in the ballast, with tubes so constructed as to convey air for his breathing. I afterwards inquired of General Savary, if there had been any foundation for such a report; when he informed me that the plan had been thought of, and the vessel in some measure prepared; but it was considered too hazardous; for had we detained the vessel for a day or two, he would have been obliged to make his situation known, and thereby forfeited all claims to the good treatment he hoped to ensure by a voluntary surrender.

The two Captains dined with me, and afterwards went on board the *Myrmidon*, to take up a position to the north-east of the *Bellerophon*, to prevent vessels from passing close in shore, and thus to render the blockade of the port more complete.

Soon after they left me, a barge was perceived rowing off from the frigates towards the *Bellerophon* with a flag-of-truce up; on which I recalled Captains Sartorius and Gambier, by signal, that they might be present at any communication that was to be made. The boat got alongside about seven p.m. and brought Count Las Cases, accompanied by General Baron Gourgaud, one of Bonaparte's Aide-de-Camps. On their coming on deck, I immediately addressed Las Cases, saying, "It is impossible you could have been at Rochefort, and returned, since you left me this morning." He replied, "No; it was not necessary; I found the Emperor at Isle d'Aix, on my arrival there." He then told me, he was charged with a letter from General Bertrand. We walked into the cabin, when he delivered it to me; it was as follows:

Le 14 Juillet, 1815.

Monsieur le Commandant,

Monsieur le Comte de Las Cases a rendu compte à l'Empereur de la conversation qu'il à eue ce matin à votre bord. S. M. se rendra à la marée de demain, vers quatre ou cinq heures du matin, à bord de votre vaisseau. Je vous envoye Monsieur le Comte de Las Cases, Conseiller d'Etât, faisant fonction de Maréchal de Logis, avec la liste des personnes composant la suite de S. M. Si l'Amiral, en conséquence de la demandé que vous lui avez adressée, vous envoys le sauf conduit demande pour les États Unis, S. M. s'y rendra avec plaisir; mais an défaut du sauf conduit, il se rendra volontiers en Angleterre, comme simple particulier, pour y jouir de la protection des loix de votre pays.

" S. M. a expédié Monsieur le Maréchal de Camp Baron Gourgaud auprès du Prince Régent, avec une lettre, dont j'ai l'honneur de vous envoyer copie, vous priant de la faire passer au Ministre auquel vous croyez nécessaire d'envoyer cet officier général, afin qu'il ait l'honneur de remettre an Prince Régent la lettre dont il est chargé.

J'ai l'honneur d'être,
    Monsieur le Commandant,
    Votre très humble et très obéissant Serviteur,
      Le Grand Maréchal,
        COMTE BERTRAND.

À Monsieur le Commandant
des Croisières devant Rochefort.

Translation

Sir,

Count Las Cases has reported to the Emperor the conversation which he had with you this morning. His Majesty will proceed on board your ship with the ebb tide tomorrow morning, between four and five o'clock.

I send the Count Las Cases, Counsellor of State, doing the duty of Maréchal de Logis, with the list of persons composing His Majesty's suite.

If the Admiral, in consequence of the despatch you forwarded to him, should send the passport for the United States therein demanded, His Majesty will be happy to repair to America; but should the passport be withheld, he will willingly proceed to England, as a private individual, there to enjoy the protection of the laws of your country.

His Majesty has despatched Major General Baron Gourgaud to the Prince Regent with a letter, a copy of which I have the honour to enclose, requesting that you will forward it to such one of the ministers as you may think it necessary to send that general officer, that he may have the honour of delivering the letter with which he is charged to the Prince Regent.

I have the honour to be, Sir,

Your very humble servant,

COUNT BERTRAND.

To the Officer commanding the
Cruizers off Rochefort

List of persons composing the suite of Napoleon Bonaparte, enclosed in the above Letter,
and the manner in which they were distributed during the passage to England.

BELLEROPHON
Généraux

Le Lieutenant Général Comte Bertrand, Gd. Maréchal.
Le Lieutenant Général Duc de Rovigo.
Le Lieutenant Général Baron Lallemand Aide de Camp de S. M.
Le Maréchal de Camp Comte de Montholon Aide de Camp de S. M.
   Le Comte de Las Cases Conseiller d'Etat.

Dames

Madame la Comtesse Bertrand.
Madame la Comtesse de Montholon.

Enfans

3 Enfans de Madame la Comtesse Bertrand.
1 Enfant de Madame la Comtesse de Montholon.

Officiers

M. de Planat, Lieutenant-Colonel.
M. Maingaut, Chirurgien de S. M.
M. Las Cases, Page.

Service de la Chambre

M. M. Marchand	1 Valet de Chambre.
Gilli	Valet de Chambre.
St Denis	Valet de Chambre.
Novarra	Idem.
Denis	Garçon de Garderobe.

Livrée

Archambaud	1 Valet de pied.
Gaudron	Valet de pied.
Gentilini	Id.

Service de la Bouche

M. M. Fontain	Maitre d'Hôtel.
Piéron	Chef d'Office.
La Fosse	Cuisinier.
Le Page	Idem.

2 Femmes de Chambre de Madame la Comtesse Bertrand.
1 Femme de Chambre de Madame la Comtesse de Montholon.

Suite des personnes qui accompagnent S. M.

1 Valet de Chambre	du Duc de Rovigo.
1 do.	du Comte Bertrand.
1 do.	du Comte de Montholon.
1 Valet de pied	du Comte Bertrand.
Total 7	

Recapitulation

Générauax	5
Dames	2
Enfans	4
Officiers	3
Service de la Chambre de S. M.	5
Livrée de S. M.	3
Service de la Bouche	4
Suite des personnes qui accompagent S. M.	7
Total	33

LA CORVETTE (HMS *Myrmidon*)
Officiers

Le Lieutenant Colonel	Resigni.
Le Lieutenant Colonel	Schultz.
Le Capitaine	Autrie.
Le Capitaine	Mesener.
Le Capitaine	Piontowski.
Le Lieutenant	Rivière.
Le Sous Lieutenant	Ste Catherine.

Suite de S. M.

Capriani	Maître d'Hôtel.
Santini	Huissier.
Chauvin	Id.
Rousseau	Lampiste.
Archambaud	Valet de pied.
Joseph	Id.
Le Charron	Id.
Lisiaux	Garde d'Office.
Ortini	Valet de pied.
Fumeau	Idem.

Recapitulation

Officiers	7
Suite	10
Total	17

Enclosed was likewise a copy of the well-known letter addressed by Bonaparte to His Royal Highness the Prince Regent.

Altesse Royale,

En butte aux factions qui divisent mon pays et à l'inimitié des plus grandes puissances de l'Europe, j'ai terminé ma carrière politique, et je viens comme Thémistocle m'asseoir sur le foyer du peuple Britannique. Je me mets sous la protection de ses loix, que je réclame de votre Altesse Royale, comme an plus puissant, au plus constant, et an plus généreux de mes Ennemis.

Rochefort, 13 Juillet, 1815,
Signé, NAPOLEON.

Translation

Rochefort, July 13th, 1815.

Your Royal Highness,

A victim to the factions which distract my country, and to the enmity of the greatest powers of Europe, I have terminated my political career, and I come, like Themistocles, to throw myself upon the hospitality of the British people. I put myself under the protection of their laws; which I claim from your Royal Highness, as the most powerful, the most constant, and the most generous of my enemies.

NAPOLEON.

On reading the above, I told Monsieur Las Cases that I would receive Bonaparte on board, and immediately forward General Gourgaud to England by the *Slaney*, along with my despatches to the Admiralty; but that he would not be allowed to land until permission was received from London, or the sanction of the Admiral at the port he might arrive at obtained. I assured him, however, that the copy of the letter with which he was charged would be forwarded without loss of time, and presented by the Ministers to his Royal Highness. Count Las Cases then asked for paper, that he might communicate by letter to Bertrand my acquiescence in the proposal he had brought, for my receiving, and conveying to England, Bonaparte and his suite.

When General Gourgaud was about to write the letter, to prevent any future misunderstanding, I said, "Monsieur Las Cases, you will recollect that I am not authorised to stipulate as to the reception of Bonaparte in England, but that he must consider himself entirely at the disposal of his Royal Highness the Prince Regent." He answered, "I am perfectly aware of that, and have already acquainted the Emperor with what you said on the subject"

It might, perhaps, have been better if this declaration had been given in an official written form; and could I have foreseen the discussions which afterwards took place, and which will appear in the sequel, I undoubtedly should have done so; but as I repeatedly made it in the presence of witnesses, it did not occur to me as being necessary; and how could a stronger proof be adduced, that no stipulations were agreed to respecting the reception of Bonaparte in England, than the fact of their not being reduced to writing? which certainly would have been the case had any favourable terms been demanded on the part of Monsieur Las Cases, and agreed to by me.

The French boat was soon after despatched with the letter to Bertrand, in charge of a French naval officer, who had attended Las Cases on board; and as soon as I had finished the following despatch to the Secretary of the Admiralty, I sent Captain Sartorius, of the *Slaney*, to England, accompanied by General Gourgaud.

Extract of a Letter from Captain Maitland, of His Majesty's ship *Bellerophon*, addressed to the Secretary of the Admiralty, dated in Basque Roads, 14th July, 1815.

> For the information of the Lords Commissioners of the Admiralty, I have to acquaint you that the Count Las Cases and General Lallemand this day came on board His Majesty's ship under my command, with a proposal from Count Bertrand for me to receive on board Napoleon Bonaparte, for the purpose of throwing himself on the generosity of the Prince Regent. Conceiving myself authorised by their Lordships' secret order, I have acceded to the proposal, and he is to embark on board this ship tomorrow morning. That no misunderstanding might arise, I have explicitly and clearly explained to Count Las Cases, that I have no authority whatever for granting terms of any sort, but that all I can do is to carry him and his suite to England, to be received in such manner as his Royal Highness may deem expedient.
>
> At Napoleon Bonaparte's request, and that their Lordships may be in possession of the transaction at as early a period as possible, I despatch the *Slaney* (with General Gourgaud, his Aide de Camp), directing Captain Sartorius to put into the nearest port, and forward this letter by his first Lieutenant, and shall in compliance with their Lordships' orders proceed to Torbay, to await such directions as the Admiralty may think proper to give.
>
> Enclosed, I transmit a copy of the letter with which General Gourgaud

is charged, to his Royal Highness the Prince Regent, and request that you will acquaint their Lordships, that the General informs me, he is entrusted with further particulars, which he is anxious to communicate to his Royal Highness.

When these gentlemen had left the ship, as well as the Saale's barge, I said to Monsieur Las Cases, I propose dividing the after-cabin in two, that the ladies may have the use of one part of it.

"If you allow me to give an opinion," said he, "the Emperor will be better pleased to have the whole of the after-cabin to himself, as he is fond of walking about, and will by that means be able to take more exercise." I answered, "As it is my wish to treat him with every possible consideration while he is on board the ship I command, I shall make any arrangement you think will be most agreeable to him."

This is the only conversation that ever passed on the subject of the cabin; and I am the more particular in stating it, as Bonaparte has been described, in some of the public Journals, as having taken possession of it in a most brutal way, saying, "Tout ou rien pour moi:"—All or nothing for me. I here therefore, once for all, beg to state most distinctly, that, from the time of his coming on board my ship, to the period of his quitting her, his conduct was invariably that of a gentleman; and in no one instance do I recollect him to have made use of a rude expression, or to have been guilty of any kind of ill-breeding.

As the ship had for some time been kept clear for action, with all the bulkheads down, it became necessary to prepare for the reception of so many guests, by putting the cabins up again: in consequence of making the requisite arrangements, it was past one o'clock in the morning before I could get to bed. About ten at night, the officer of the watch informed me that a boat from the shore had asked permission to come alongside. A man being allowed to come on board from her; "I am sent off from Rochelle," said he, "to inform you that Bonaparte this morning passed that town in a chasse-marée, with another in company, for the purpose of escaping to sea by the Pertuis de Breton: he is now in that passage, and means to set sail this night." I told him, "that I doubted his information, having at that moment one of his attendants on board, who had come with a proposal for me to receive him into the ship. I then asked him how he came by his intelligence?" He answered, "The vessels passed close to a boat that I was in; and I saw a man wrapt up in a sailor's great coat, whom one of the people with me asserted to be him: for my part, I am not acquainted with his appearance, never having seen him; but when the owner of the vessels attempted to go on board of them, he was kept off, and told that they were required for two or three days, when they would be restored with ample payment." He told his story so circumstantially, and with such confidence, that I feared there must be grounds for what he stated; and the anxiety of my situation may be easily conceived, when it is recollected that I had sent off a ship to England with despatches, announcing the intention of Bonaparte to embark the following morning in the *Bellerophon*. After a little consideration, I determined to inform Las Cases abruptly of the intelligence I had received, and endeavour to judge by the effect it had on his countenance, whether there was any truth in the report or not. I accordingly went into the cabin and did so; he seemed perfectly calm and collected, saying, "Pray at what hour does your informant state the Emperor to have passed Rochelle?" "At ten a.m." "Then I can safely assert, on my honour, that he was not in either of those vessels. I left him at half-past five this evening, when it was his full intention to come on board this ship tomorrow morning; what he may have done since that hour, I cannot be responsible for." I answered, "As you give your word of honour that Bonaparte had not left Isle d'Aix when you quitted it, I shall trust to what you say, and take no steps in consequence of the information that has been brought to me, but conclude it has originated in some mistake."

About three in the morning, the officer of the watch awoke me, and said that another boat wished to come alongside. I rose and went upon deck immediately, and found that she brought the same intelligence from another quarter; and they both eventually proved correct, to a certain extent: for two chasse-marées, as I was afterwards informed, had been prepared, manned, and officered from the frigates, to be used as a last resource to attempt an escape in, in the event of Las Cases' mission to the *Bellerophon* not being successful; and they had actually passed Rochelle, in their way to Pointeau d'Aguillon, at the hour specified, and were there to await his joining them should it prove necessary." Chasse-Marées are small decked vessels, rigged as luggers; they are generally from twenty to thirty-five tons burthen, and are used almost exclusively for the coasting trade of France. Though there is no doubt that, during the summer months, a vessel of this description might succeed in making the voyage to America; yet if we take into consideration the indolent habits that Bonaparte had of late years given way to; the very small space for the accommodation of himself and suite, and for the stowage of provisions, water, and other necessaries; that there was no friendly port he could have touched at, to gain supplies; the utter impracticability of his reaching his destination in a vessel of that description, even if he had eluded the vigilance of our cruisers, will at once be evident to everyone.

After I had determined to abide by Las Cases' assurance, that Bonaparte had not quitted Isle d'Aix, I enquired of the person who brought off the information in the evening, "What was the state of Rochelle, and whether I might with safety send a boat there to purchase refreshments?" as the white flag was then hoisted all over the town; he said, "he would not recommend it, as, though the towns-people were well inclined towards the Bourbon family, the garrison, consisting of four thousand men, were all attached to Bonaparte; but if he were once on board the ship, there would be no risk in doing so, as their fear of his meeting with bad treatment would keep the soldiers in awe.

3

The Journey to England on HMS *Bellerophon*

At break of day, on 15th July, 1815, *l'Epervier* French brig of war was discovered under sail, standing out towards the ship, with a flag of truce up; and at the same time the *Superb*, bearing Sir Henry Hotham's flag, was seen in the offing. By half-past five the ebb-tide failed, the wind was blowing right in, and the brig, which was within a mile of us, made no further progress; while the *Superb* was advancing with the wind and tide in her favour. Thus situated, and being most anxious to terminate the affair I had brought so near a conclusion, previous to the Admiral's arrival, I sent off Mr Mott, the First Lieutenant, in the barge, who returned soon after six o'clock, bringing Napoleon with him.

On coming on board the *Bellerophon*, he was received without any of the honours generally paid to persons of high rank; the guard was drawn out on the break of the poop, but did not present arms. His Majesty's Government had merely given directions, in the event of his being captured, for his being removed into any one of his Majesty's ships that might fall in with him; but no instructions had been given as to the light, in which he was to be viewed. As it is not customary, however, on board a British ship of war, to pay any such honours before the colours are hoisted at eight o'clock in the morning, or after sunset, I made the early hour an excuse for withholding them upon this occasion.

Bonaparte's dress was an olive-coloured great coat over a green uniform, with scarlet cape and cuffs, green lapels turned back and edged with scarlet, skirts hooked back with bugle horns embroidered in gold, plain sugar-loaf buttons and gold epaulettes; being the uniform of the Chasseur à Cheval of the Imperial Guard. He wore the star, or grand cross of the Legion of Honour, and the small cross of that order; the Iron Crown; and the Union, appended to the button-hole of his left lapel. He had on a small cocked hat, with a tricoloured cockade; plain gold-hilted sword, military boots, and white waistcoat and

Napoleon embarking on the *Bellerophon* from a drawing by Jean-Jérôme Beaugean.

breeches. The following day he appeared in shoes, with gold buckles, and silk stockings—the dress he always wore afterwards, while with me.

On leaving the *Epervier*, he was cheered by her ship's company as long as the boat was within hearing; and Mr Mott informed me that most of the officers and men had tears in their eyes.

General Bertrand came first up the ship's side, and said to me, "The Emperor is in the boat." He then ascended, and, when he came on the quarter-deck, pulled off his hat, and, addressing me in a firm tone of voice, said, "I am come to throw myself on the protection of your Prince and laws." When I showed him into the cabin, he looked round and said, "Une belle chambre," "This is a handsome cabin." I answered, "Such as it is, Sir, it is at your service while you remain on board the ship I command." He then looked at a portrait that was hanging up, and said, "Qui est cette jeune personne?" "Who is that young lady?" "My wife," I replied. "Ah! elle est très jeune et très jolie," "Ah! she is both young and pretty." He then asked what countrywoman she was, begged to know if I had any children, and put a number of questions respecting my country, and the service I had seen. He next requested I would send for the officers, and introduce them to him: which was done according to their rank. He asked several questions of each, as to the place of his birth, the situation he held in the ship, the length of time he had served, and the actions he had been in. He then expressed a desire to go round the ship; but, as the men had not done cleaning, I told him it was customary to clean the lower decks immediately after their breakfast, that they were then so employed, and, if he would defer visiting the ship until they had finished, he would see her to more advantage.

At this time I proposed to him to allow me to address him in English, as I had heard he understood that language, and I had considerable difficulty in expressing myself in French. He replied in French, "The thing is impossible; I hardly understand a word of your language:" and from the observations I had an opportunity of making afterwards, I am satisfied he made a correct statement, as, on looking into books or newspapers, he frequently asked the meaning of the most common word. He spoke his own language with a rapidity that at first made it difficult to follow him; and it was several days before I got so far accustomed to his manner of speaking, as to comprehend his meaning immediately.

In about a quarter of an hour, he again intimated a desire to go round the ship; and although I told him he would find the men rubbing and scouring, he persisted in his wish of seeing her in the state she then was. He accordingly went over all her decks, asking me many questions; more particularly about anything that appeared to him different from what he had been accustomed to see in French ships of war. He seemed most struck with the cleanliness and neatness of the men, saying "that our seamen were surely a different class of people from the French; and that he thought it was owing to them we were always victorious at sea." I answered, "I must beg leave to differ with you: I do not wish to take from the merit of our men; but my own opinion is, that perhaps we owe our advantage to the superior experience of the officers; and I believe the French seamen, if taken as much pains with, would look as well as ours. As British ships of war are constantly at sea, the officers have nothing to divert their attention from them and their men; and in consequence, not only is their appearance more attended to, but they are much better trained to the service they have to perform."

"I believe you are right," said he. He then went on to talk of several naval actions; adding, "Your laws are either more severe, or better administered, than ours; there are many instances of French officers having conducted themselves ill in battle, without my being able to punish them as they deserved:" among others, he mentioned the names of two naval officers; and speaking of one of them, said, " He ought to have suffered death, and I did all I could to bring it about, but he was tried by a French naval court-martial, which only dismissed him the service." I observed, "The laws appear sometimes to be administered with more than sufficient severity. I commanded a frigate in the affair of Basque Roads; and in my opinion, the sentence of death on the Captain of the *Calcutta* was unjust: he could do no more to save his ship, and she was defended better and longer than any one there." He answered, "You are not aware of the circumstances that occasioned his condemnation; he was the first man to quit his ship, which was fought some time by her officers and crew after he had left her."

He next said, "I can see no sufficient reason why your ships should beat the French with so much ease. The finest men of war in your service are French; a French ship is heavier in every respect than one of yours, she carries more guns, those guns of a larger calibre, and has a great many more men." I replied, "I have already accounted for it to you, in the superior experience of our men and officers." "I understand," said he, "from some Frenchmen who were on board your ship for several days, that you take great pains in exercising your guns, and training your men to fire at a mark." These men were part of the officers and crew of the *Æneas* store-ship, mentioned as having been detained on the 18th of June, who were on board the *Bellerophon* about a week, and were landed at Isle d'Aix, in a chasse-marée, a few days before Bonaparte's arrival there. I answered, "I did so, because I considered it of the greatest importance;" and I added, "that if the frigates had attempted to put to sea, he would probably have had an opportunity of seeing the effect of it." He asked me "if I thought two frigates, with four-and-twenty pounders on their main decks, were a match for a seventy-four gun ship; and whether it was my opinion, if he had attempted to force a passage in the ships at Isle d'Aix, it would have been attended with success." I replied, "that the fire of a two-deck ship was so much more compact, and carried such an immense weight of iron, in proportion to that of a frigate, and there was so much difficulty in bringing two or three ships to act with effect at the same time upon one, that I scarcely considered three frigates a match for one line-of-battle ship;—that, with respect to forcing a passage past the *Bellerophon*, it must have depended greatly on accident, but the chances were much against it; as the frigates would have had to beat out against the wind for three or four leagues, through a narrow passage, exposed to the fire of a seventy-four gun ship, which, from being to windward, would have had the power of taking the position most advantageous for herself." He then said, reverting to what had passed before about firing at marks, "You have a great advantage over France in your finances: I have long wished to introduce the use of powder and shot in exercise; but the expense was too great for the country to bear." He examined the sights on the guns, and approved of them highly; asked the weight of metal on the different decks, disapproving of the mixture of different calibres on the quarter-deck and forecastle. I told him the long nines were placed in the way of the rigging, that they might carry the fire from the explosion clear of it, which a carronade would not do: he answered, "That may be necessary, but it must be attended with inconvenience." His enquiries were generally much to the purpose, and showed that he had given naval matters a good deal of consideration.

On seeing the additional supply of wads for each deck made up along with the shotboxes, in the form of sophas, with neat canvas covers, he observed, "The French ships of war have all the preparations for action that you have, but they have not the way of combining appearance with utility."

We had breakfast about nine o'clock, in the English style, consisting of tea, coffee, cold meat, &c. He did not eat much, or seem to relish it; and when, on enquiry, I found he was accustomed to have a hot meal in the morning, I immediately ordered my steward to allow his Maître d'Hôtel to give directions, that he might invariably be served in the manner he had been used to; and after that we always lived in the French fashion, as far as I could effect that object.

During breakfast he asked many questions about English customs, saying, "I must now learn to conform myself to them, as I shall probably pass the remainder of my life in England."

The *Superb*, as I before observed, had been seen in the offing early in the morning, and was now approaching with a light breeze: he asked two or three times how soon she would anchor, seemed very anxious to know whether the Admiral would approve of my having received him; and when I went to wait on Sir Henry Hotham, requested I would say he was desirous of seeing him.

The *Superb* anchored about half-past ten, and I immediately went on board, and gave the Admiral an account of all that had occurred, adding, "I trust I have done right, and that the Government will approve of my conduct, as I considered it of much importance to prevent Bonaparte's escape to America, and to get possession of his person." Sir Henry Hotham said, "Getting hold of him on any terms would have been of the greatest consequence; but as you have entered into no conditions whatever, there cannot be a doubt that you will obtain the approbation of his Majesty's Government."

He then said, "How do you feel as to keeping him? would you like to part with him?" "Certainly not," was my answer: "as I have had all the anxiety and responsibility of conducting this matter to an issue, I am of course desirous of taking him to England; but, as I do not wish to keep him, or any man, in my ship against his will, if he desires to remove into another, I shall certainly not object."

I then delivered Bonaparte's message, that he was desirous of receiving a visit from the Admiral, who said he would wait upon him with much pleasure.

I soon after returned to the *Bellerophon*, and told Bonaparte that the Admiral meant to wait on him; upon which he desired Count Bertrand to go and pay his respects to Sir Henry. I accompanied him, and while the Admiral was preparing for his visit, Captain Senhouse attended General Bertrand through the ship.

In the afternoon, Sir Henry Hotham, accompanied by Captain Senhouse, and Mr Irving, his secretary, came on board the *Bellerophon*. They were introduced to Bonaparte by General Bertrand, in the after-cabin, where he had a good deal of conversation with them: he showed his portable library, which was laid out in small travelling cases round the cabin; asked various questions, principally relative to the discipline and regulation of our ships of war, and finally invited them all to remain to dinner.

Dinner was served about five o'clock upon Bonaparte's plate. This was arranged by his Maître d'Hôtel, whom I had told to regulate everything in the manner most likely to be agreeable to his master.

When dinner was announced, Bonaparte, viewing himself as a Royal personage, which he continued to do while on board the *Bellerophon*, and which, under the circumstances, I considered it would have been both ungracious and uncalled for in me to have disputed, led the way into the dining-room. He seated himself in the centre at one side of the table, requesting Sir Henry Hotham to sit at his right hand, and Madame Bertrand on his left. For that day I sat as usual at the head of the table, but on the following day, and every other, whilst Bonaparte remained on board, I sat by his request at his right hand, and General Bertrand took the top. Two of the ward-room officers dined daily at the table, by invitation from Bonaparte, conveyed through Count Bertrand.

He conversed a great deal, and showed no depression of spirits: among other things, he asked me where I was born. I told him, in Scotland. "Have you any property there?" said he. "No, I am a younger brother, and they do not bestow much on people of that description in Scotland." "Is your elder brother a Lord?" "No, Lord Lauderdale is the head of our family." "Ah! you are a relation of Lord Lauderdale's! he is an acquaintance of mine, he was sent Ambassador from your King to me, when Mr Fox was Prime Minister: had Mr Fox lived, it never would have come to this, but his death put an end to all hopes of peace. Milord Lauderdale est un bon garçon;" adding, "I think you resemble him a little, though he is dark and you are fair."

When dinner was over, a cup of strong coffee was handed round; he then rose and went into the after-cabin, asking the Admiral and all the party to accompany him, the ladies among the rest. This was the only time I ever saw them in the apartment in which he slept.

After some conversation, he said, in a cheerful and playful way, that he would show us his camp bed; and sent for Marchand, his premier valet de chambre, who received his order, and soon returned with two small packages in leather cases; one of which contained the bedstead, which was composed of steel, and, when packed up, was not above two feet long and eighteen inches in circumference; the other contained the mattress and curtains, the latter of green silk. In three minutes the whole was put together, and formed a very elegant small bed, about thirty inches wide.

He then went out, and walked the quarter-deck for some time, and retired to his cabin about half-past seven o'clock. Soon after, when the Admiral was going to return to his ship, he proposed to Bertrand to take leave of him. He went into the cabin, but returned immediately with an apology, saying he was undressed, and going to bed.

In the course of the afternoon, the Admiral invited Bonaparte, with the ladies and all his principal officers, to breakfast, the following day: which invitation was accepted, apparently, with much satisfaction.

When I went on deck, early the next morning, (the 16th of July) I observed that the *Superb* had the tompions out of her guns, and the man ropes on her yards, as if for the purpose of saluting and manning ships; and as I had received Bonaparte without even the guard presenting arms, I felt that he might conceive I had intentionally treated him with disrespect. I therefore sent the officer of the watch with my compliments to Sir Henry Hotham, and begged to know if it was his intention to salute Bonaparte on his going on board, and to receive him with manned yards; and, if so, whether I was to do the same, on his quitting the *Bellerophon*. He sent for answer, that it was not his intention to salute, but he meant to man ship; that I was not to do so on his quitting the *Bellerophon*, but was at liberty to man yards on his return. I likewise received directions from the Admiral to hoist a signal, when the boat with his visitors was ready to leave the ship, that he might have time to make the necessary preparations.

About ten a.m. the barge was manned, and a captain's guard turned out. When Bonaparte came on deck, he looked at the marines, who were generally fine-looking young men, with much satisfaction; went through their ranks, inspected their arms, and admired their appearance, saying to Bertrand, "How much might be done with a hundred thousand such soldiers as these." He asked which had been longest in the corps; went up and spoke to him. His questions were put in French, which I interpreted, as well as the man's answers. He enquired how many years he had served; on being told upwards of ten, he turned to me and said, "Is it not customary in your service, to give a man who has been in it so long some mark of distinction?" He was informed that the person in question had been a sergeant, but was reduced to the ranks for some misconduct. He then put the guard through part of their exercise, whilst I interpreted to the Captain of Marines, who did not understand French, the manoeuvres he wished to have performed. He made some remarks upon the difference of the charge with the bayonet between our troops and the French; and found fault with our method of fixing the bayonet to the musquet, as being

A sketch taken on *Bellerophon*
by Colonel Planat, a member of
Napoleon's entourage. Colonel Planat
de Fraye was an aide-de-camp and
orderly officer.

more easy to twist off, if seized by an enemy when in the act of charging.

On getting into the boat, he looked at the barge's crew, and said, "What a very fine set of men you have got!" He then turned to Las Cases, who had come on board the ship in plain clothes, but now appeared in a naval uniform, and said jocularly, "Comment, Las Cases, vous êtes militaire?" "What, Las Cases, are you a military man? I have never till now seen you in uniform." He answered, "Please your Majesty, before the revolution I was a lieutenant in the navy; and as I think an uniform carries more consideration with it in a foreign country, I have adopted it."

His attention was now drawn to the men on the *Superb*'s yards, as well as to the appearance of the ship, about which he made some observations, and asked several questions; among others, whether she was French or English; what her age was; the number of guns she carried, and the weight of metal on each deck.

On going alongside, General Bertrand went up and announced to the Admiral, that the Emperor, for they always gave him that title, was in the boat. He then went up, and was received by Sir Henry Hotham on the quarter-deck, where a captain's guard was turned out to him. He was immediately shown into the cabin, and, after looking round him, requested to have the officers presented, which was done; when he asked nearly the same questions of each, that he had put to those of the *Bellerophon* the day before. He then expressed a wish to go through the ship; and did so, accompanied by several of his own suite, the Admiral, Captain Senhouse, and myself. The men were drawn up at divisions, and everything was in the nicest order. He appeared much pleased with all he saw, and drew many comparisons between French and English ships of war. On going through the wings and storerooms, he said to General Savary, "Our ships have nothing of this sort:" who answered, "All the new ones, built at Antwerp, were constructed on this plan." When he returned to the quarter-deck, he questioned the Admiral and myself very minutely, about the clothing and victualing of the seamen. It was then, on being told that all that department was under the charge of the purser, he said in a facetious way, "Je crois que c'est quelquefois chez vous, comme chez nous, le commissaire est un pen coquin." "I believe it happens sometimes with you, as it does with us, that the purser is a little of a rogue." This was addressed to the Admiral and me, with whom he was conversing, and not to the people, as has been represented; nor was there a man that could have understood it, as it was spoken in French, and not within their hearing. He asked to see the Chaplain, put a few questions to him as to the number of Catholics and foreigners in the ship, and whether any of them spoke the French language. A Guernsey man was pointed out to him, but he had no conversation with him.

He was then shown into the cabin, where breakfast was prepared: during which meal he talked a good deal, but ate little, the breakfast being served in the English manner. I observed, during the whole time of breakfast, that Colonel Planat, who was much attached to him, and of whom Bonaparte always expressed himself in terms of affection, had tears running down his cheeks, and seemed greatly distressed at the situation of his master. And, from the opportunities I afterwards had of observing this young man's character, I feel convinced he had a strong personal attachment to Bonaparte; and this, indeed, as far as I could judge, was the case also with all his other attendants, without exception.

On rising from the breakfast-table, the whole party went into the after-cabin, where a discussion took place about Bonaparte's horses and carriages, which had been left at Rochefort, and which he was desirous of having forwarded to England. I had formerly agreed, in the event of their arriving, to receive two carriages, and five or six horses, as many as the ship could conveniently stow; but as they had not come, the Admiral now consented to give a passport for a vessel to transport the whole of them, consisting of six carriages and forty-five horses: which was accordingly made out, and forwarded to Monsieur Philibert, the senior naval officer at Isle d'Aix, but I believe it was never acted upon.

We all returned to the *Bellerophon* about noon, when the ships present manned their yards, the boat was immediately hoisted in, and the ship got under weigh, in pursuance of orders from the Admiral, of which the following is an extract.

Extract of an Order from Rear Admiral Sir Henry Hotham, KCB, addressed to Captain Maitland of HMS *Bellerophon*, dated *Superb*, in Basque Roads, July 15th, 1815.

> You are hereby required and directed to take the *Myrmidon* under your orders, and, putting on board her such persons composing a part of the suite of Napoleon Bonaparte as cannot be conveyed in the *Bellerophon*, you are to put to sea in HMS under your command, in company with the *Myrmidon*, and make the best of your way with Napoleon Bonaparte and his suite to Torbay, and there landing the officer of the ship bearing my flag, whom I have charged with a despatch addressed to the Secretary of the Admiralty, as well as an officer of the ship you command, for the purpose of proceeding express to Plymouth with the despatch you will herewith receive, addressed to Admiral Lord Keith, and a copy of these instructions (which you will transmit to his Lordship,) await orders from the Lords Commissioners of the Admiralty, or his Lordship, for your further proceedings.

During the time we were heaving the anchor up, and setting the sails, Bonaparte remained on the break of the poop; and was very inquisitive about what was going on. He observed, "Your method of performing this manoeuvre is quite different from the French;" and added, "What I admire most in your ship, is the extreme silence and orderly conduct of your men:—on board a French ship, everyone calls and gives orders, and they gabble like so many geese." Previous to his quitting the *Bellerophon* he made the same remark, saying, "There has been less noise in this ship, where there are six hundred men, during the whole of the time I have been in her, than there was on board the *Epervier*, with only one hundred, in the passage from Isle d'Aix to Basque Roads."

Soon after the ship was under weigh, the *Mouche* joined, with three or four sheep, a quantity of vegetables, and other refreshments,—a present from the French Commodore to Bonaparte. After receiving them on board, we made sail, accompanied by the *Myrmidon*, for England.

In working out, we passed within about a cable's length of the *Superb*. He asked me if I considered that was near enough for a naval engagement: I answered, that half the distance, or even less, would suit much better; as it was a maxim in our navy, not to be further from our enemy than to give room for working the yards, and manoeuvring the ship.

He remained upon deck all the time the ship was beating out of the Pertuis d'Antioche. Having cleared the Chasseron shoal about six p.m., dinner was served. He conversed a great deal at table, and seemed in very good spirits; told several anecdotes of himself; among others, one relating to Sir Sydney Smith. Knowing that I had served under that officer on the coast of Syria, he turned to me and said, "Did Sir Sydney Smith ever tell you the cause of his quarrel with me?" I answered he had not. "Then," said he, "I will.—When the French army was before St Jean d'Acre, he had a paper privately distributed among the officers and soldiers, tending to induce them to revolt and quit me; on which I issued a proclamation, denouncing the English commanding-officer as a madman, and prohibiting all intercourse with him. This nettled Sir Sydney so much, that he sent me a challenge to meet him in single combat on the beach at Caiffa. My reply was, that when Marlborough appeared for that purpose, I should be at his service; but I had other duties to fulfil besides fighting a duel with an English commodore." He pursued the subject of Syria, and said, patting me (who was sitting next him) on the head; "If it had not been for you English, I should have been Emperor of the East; but wherever there is water to float a ship, we are sure to find you in our way.

During the 17th and 18th of July, the weather was very fine, and nothing of note occurred. Several strange vessels were seen, about which Bonaparte and his attendants were very inquisitive, in order, I presume, that they might judge whether they would probably have escaped or not, had they put to sea. The only ship of war fallen in with on those days was the *Bacchus* sloop, which I pointed out; and at the same time informed him, that we had several frigates cruising in this position, for the purpose of intercepting him, had he got past the ships stationed close in with the land. This, as it afterward appeared, was not the case: the *Endymion* having gone into the Gironde, the *Liffey* having sprung her bowsprit and returned to England, and the others, from various causes, having quitted the station; so that, had he passed the squadron off Rochefort, there can be little doubt he would have made his voyage in safety to America.

About this time, Bonaparte amused himself by playing at cards after breakfast: the game was vingt-un, in which all the party joined, except myself. He proposed that I should play with them, but I told him I had no money, making it a rule to leave it all with my wife before I went to sea: on which he laughed, and good-humouredly offered to lend me some, and trust me until we arrived in England: I, however, declined his offer, having the numerous duties of the ship to attend to.

As my despatch of the 14th instant to the Secretary of the Admiralty had been very short, and written in great haste, being desirous that his Majesty's Ministers should be made acquainted with the important arrangements agreed upon, as early as possible, I considered it right to make a more detailed report to the Commander in Chief; and therefore wrote a despatch to Lord Keith, of which the following are extracts, intending to send it by the officer who should announce to him the *Bellerophon*'s arrival in Torbay.

Napoleon on board HMS *Bellerophon;* detail from a painting by Sir William Quiller Orchardson. From left to right: Colonel Planat, (a member of Napoleon's suite); Charles Tristan, Comte de Montholon, (secretary, ambassador and long-serving confidante to Napoleon); Pierre Maingaut, (Napoleon's surgeon); Emanuel Auguste Dieudonné Marius Joseph, Marquis Las Cases, (secretary); General Anne Jean Marie René Savary, 1st Duc de Rovigo, (a member of Napoleon's suite); General Charles François Antoine Lallemand, (a member of Napoleon's suite); General Henri Gratien Comte de Bertrand, (Grand Marshal of the Chamber); Emanuel Pons Dieudonné, (later Comte de) Las Cases, (son of the marquis) and Napoleon Bonaparte. Of these, Planat, Maingaut, Savary and Lallemand did not trans-ship to HMS *Northumberland* for the onward journey to St Helena.

Extract of a Letter from Captain Maitland, addressed to Admiral Viscount Keith, GCB, dated on hoard HM Ship *Bellerophon*, at sea, July 18th, 1815.

Having received directions from Sir Henry Hotham to forward the accompanying despatch to your Lordship by an officer, I avail myself of the opportunity to explain the circumstances under which I was placed when induced to receive Napoleon Bonaparte into the ship I command.

After the first communication was made to me by Count Bertrand (a copy of which, with my answer, has been forwarded to your Lordship by Sir Henry Hotham) that Bonaparte was at Isle d'Aix, and actually embarked on board the frigates for the purpose of proceeding to the United States of America, my duty became peculiarly harassing and anxious, owing to the numerous reports, that were daily brought from all quarters, of his intention to escape in vessels of various descriptions, and from different situations on the coast, of which the limited means I possessed, together with the length of time requisite to communicate with Sir Henry Hotham at Quiberon Bay, rendered the success at least possible, and even probable. Thus situated, the enemy having two frigates and a brig, while the force under my command consisted of the *Bellerophon* and *Slaney* (having detached the *Myrmidon* to reinforce the *Daphne* off the Mamusson passage, where the force was considerably superior to her, and whence one of the reports stated Bonaparte meant to sail,) another flag of truce was sent out, for the ostensible reason of enquiring whether I had received an answer to the former, but I soon ascertained the real one to be a proposal from Bonaparte to embark for England in this ship.

Taking into consideration all the circumstances of the probability of the escape being effected, if the trial was made either in the frigates, or clandestinely in a small vessel, as, had this ship been disabled in action, there was no other with me that could produce any effect on a frigate, and, from the experience I have had in blockading the ports of the bay, knowing the impossibility of preventing small vessels from getting to sea, and looking upon it as of the greatest importance to get possession of the person of Bonaparte; I was induced, without hesitation, to accede to the proposal, as far as taking him on board, and proceeding with him to England: but, at the same time, stating in the most clear and positive terms, that I had no authority to make any sort of stipulation as to the reception he was to meet with.

I am happy to say, that the measures I have adopted have met with the approbation of Sir Henry Hotham, and will, I trust and hope, receive that of your Lordship, as well as of his Majesty's Government.

On the 19th, a conversation took place between Madame Bertrand and myself, about Bonaparte's voyage to Elba. She asked me if I was acquainted with Captain Usher. On my answering in the negative, she said, "The Emperor is very fond of him: he gave him his portrait set with diamonds, and has another which he intends for you." I replied, "I hope not, as I cannot accept of it. Captain Usher's situation and mine were very different, and what might be proper in him would not be so in me." She rejoined, "If you do not accept of it, you will offend him very much." "If that is the case," I said, "I shall be obliged to you to take steps to prevent its being offered, as I wish to save him the mortification, and myself the pain, of a refusal; and I feel it absolutely impossible, situated as I am, to take a present from him. In receiving him on board, I had no direct authority from my Government, and I have yet to learn whether my conduct will be approved of. Besides, were I to receive a present of such value, it might possibly be said, that I was actuated by selfish motives; whereas all the measures I have taken were dictated solely by the desire of serving my country to the best of my judgment: if, therefore, I am to receive any reward, it must come from that quarter."

On the 20th of July, early in the morning, we spoke the *Swiftsure*, on her way from England to reinforce me in the blockade of Rochefort. The astonishment of Captain Webley can scarcely be conceived, when, on his entering the ship, I said, "Well, I have got him." "Got him! got whom?" "Why, Bonaparte; the man that has been keeping all Europe in a ferment these last twenty years." "Is it possible?" said he; "well, you are a lucky fellow." We had some further conversation; but Captain Webley was not introduced to Bonaparte, who had not then left his cabin; and as the *Swiftsure* was going to the southward, and I was desirous of getting to England as quickly as possible, we soon parted company.

During the 21st and 22nd of July, we exchanged signals with two or three others of our ships, which I took care to explain were on the look-out for my guest; and he seemed by this time pretty well convinced that an attempt to elude our cruisers would have been fruitless. On the latter day, the *Prometheus* showed her number, while we were at dinner: when Bonaparte expressed a wish to know whether the ships at Brest had hoisted the white flag or not. I sent for the officer of the watch, and desired him to ask the question by telegraph. In a few minutes he returned, with an answer in the affirmative. Bonaparte made no remark upon this information; but asked, with apparent indifference, how the question and answer had been conveyed; and when I explained it to him, he approved highly of the usefulness of the invention.

During meals, he always entered very freely and familiarly into conversation with those about him, addressing himself frequently to Las Cases and me; asking many questions about the manners, customs, and laws of the English; often repeating the observation he had made on first coming on board, that he must gain all the information possible on those subjects, and conform himself to them, as he should probably end his life among that people. Monsieur Las Cases, it appears, had emigrated from France early in the revolution, and remained in England until the peace of Amiens, when he was allowed to return to his own country.

Sunday, the 23rd of July, we passed very near to Ushant: the day was fine, and Bonaparte remained upon deck great part of the morning. He cast many a melancholy look at the coast of France, but made few observations on it. He asked several questions about the coast of England; whether it was safe to approach; its distance, and the part we were likely to make. About eight in the evening, the high land of Dartmoor was discovered, when I went into the cabin and told him of it: I found him in a flannel dressing-gown, nearly undressed, and preparing to go to bed. He put on his great-coat, came out upon deck, and remained some time looking at the land; asking its distance from Torbay, and the probable time of our arrival there.

4

At Torbay and Plymouth

At daybreak of the 24th of July, we were close off Dartmouth. Count Bertrand went into the cabin, and informed Bonaparte of it, who came upon deck about half-past four, and remained on the poop until the ship anchored in Torbay. He talked with admiration of the boldness of the coast; saying, "You have in that respect a great advantage over France, which is surrounded by rocks and dangers." On opening Torbay, he was much struck with the beauty of the scenery; and exclaimed, "What a beautiful country! it very much resembles the bay of Porto Ferrajo, in Elba."

The ship was scarcely at anchor, when an officer came alongside, bringing an order from Lord Keith; of which I give an extract.

Extract of an Order from Admiral Viscount Keith, GCB, addressed to Captain Maitland, of HMS *Bellerophon*, dated Ville de Paris, Hamoaze, 23rd July, 1815.

Captain Sartorius, of His Majesty's ship *Slaney*, delivered to me last night, at eleven o'clock, your despatch of the 14th instant, acquainting me that Bonaparte had proposed to embark on board the ship you command; and that you had acceded thereto, with the intention of proceeding to Torbay, there to wait for further orders. I lost no time in forwarding your letter by Captain Sartorius to the Lords Commissioners of the Admiralty, in order that their Lordships might, through him, be acquainted with every circumstance that had occurred on an occasion of so much importance; and you may expect orders from their Lordships for your further guidance. You are to, remain in Torbay until you receive such orders; and in the meantime, in addition to the directions already in your possession, you are most positively ordered to prevent every person whatever from coming on board the ship you command, except the officers and men who compose her crew;

nor is any person whatever, whether in His Majesty's service or not, who does not belong to the ship, to be suffered to come on board, either for the purpose of visiting the officers, or on any pretence whatever, without express permission either from the Lords Commissioners of the Admiralty, or from me. As I understand from Captain Sartorius, that General Gourgaud refused to deliver the letter with which he was charged for the Prince Regent, to any person except his Royal Highness, you are to take him out of the *Slaney*, into the ship you command, until you receive directions from the Admiralty on the subject, and order that ship back to Plymouth Sound, when Captain Sartorius returns from London.

Along with the above order, I received a letter from Lord Keith, of which I give some extracts.

> You will perceive by the newspapers, that the intelligence had reached London before Captain Sartorius, owing to his long passage. I have a letter from Lord Melville today, enforcing in the strongest manner the former orders, even that no person, myself or Sir John Duckworth excepted, shall be suffered to come on board the ship, till orders are sent from Government; which you will be so good as strictly to comply with. Let him and his want for nothing; and send to me for anything Brixham cannot furnish; I will send it to you by a small vessel. You may say to Napoleon, that I am under the greatest personal obligations to him for his attention to my nephew, who was taken and brought before him at Belle Alliance, and who must have died, if he had not ordered a surgeon to dress him immediately, and sent him to a hut. I am glad it fell into your hands at this time, because a Frenchman had been sent from Paris on the mission, a Monsieur Drigni.

Bonaparte recollected the circumstance alluded to, and seemed much gratified with Lord Keith's acknowledgments.

Napoleon and all his attendants were very anxious to see as many newspapers as possible, but particularly the *Courier*, which they considered the Ministerial paper, and most likely to contain the intentions of Government respecting them. They received little encouragement from any of them, but least of all from those which are supposed to take the Ministerial side in politics, as they not only contained a great deal that was personally offensive, but stated, in very plain terms, that none of the party would be allowed to land in England, and that St Helena was the probable place of their ultimate destination. Bonaparte himself always affected to consider this as a mere newspaper report, though I believe it gave him a good deal of uneasiness. His followers received it with much irritation and impatience, frequently endeavouring to convince me that our Government could have no right to dispose of them in that way, and talking to me, as if I had been one of his Majesty's Ministers, and had influence in determining on their future destination. All I could say on the subject did not prevent them from frequently recurring to it, and appealing against the injustice of such a measure.

This morning General Gourgaud returned from the *Slaney*, which we found lying here, not having been permitted to land, and having refused to deliver the letter he had been charged with for the Prince Regent to any person except his Royal Highness himself.

When I was conversing with Madame Bertrand, she said, "Had the Emperor gained the battle of Waterloo, he would have been firmly seated on the throne of France." I answered, "It certainly might have protracted his downfall, but, in all probability, he would have been overthrown at last, as the Russians were fast advancing, and he never could have resisted the combined forces of the Allies." To which she replied, "If your army had been defeated, the Russians never would have acted against him." "That I cannot believe," I said, "as they were using every effort to join and support the Allies; and the assertion is ridiculous." "Ah," said she, "you may laugh at it, and so may other people, nor will it, perhaps, now be discovered; but remember what I say, and be assured that at some future period it will be proved, that it never was Alexander's intention to cross the frontiers of France, in opposition to him."

In the course of the day I received many applications for admittance into the ship: among others a note from a lady residing in the neighbourhood, accompanied by a basket of fruit, requesting a boat might be sent for her next morning. I returned a civil answer, informing her that my instructions would not admit of her request being complied with: no more fruit was sent from that quarter. Lord Gwydir and Lord Charles Bentinck also applied for admittance, but with no better success.

No sooner was Bonaparte's arrival known in the neighbourhood, than the ship was surrounded by a crowd of boats, people being drawn from all quarters to see this extraordinary man. He came often upon deck, and showed himself at the gangways and stern windows, apparently for the purpose of gratifying their curiosity, of which, as he observed to me, the English appeared to have a very large portion.

In the evening, the officer who had been sent to Plymouth, on the ship's arrival, with despatches for Lord Keith, returned, bringing letters, from which I give the following extracts:

Extract of a Letter from Admiral Viscount Keith, GCB, addressed to Captain Maitland, of HMS *Bellerophon*, dated Ville de Paris, Hamoaze, July 24, 1815.

The officer of the ship you command has just delivered to me your letter of this date, reporting your arrival in Torbay, with the Bellerophon and Myrmidon, having on board Napoleon Bonaparte and his suite. I have also received your other letter, explaining the circumstances under which you were placed, when you were induced to receive Napoleon on board; and I shall transmit the same to the Lords Commissioners of the Admiralty, in confident expectation, that his Majesty's Government will fully approve of your conduct.

Extract of a Letter from Admiral Viscount Keith, GCB, addressed to Captain Maitland, of HMS *Bellerophon*, dated 24th July, 1815.

I take the opportunity of your officer's return, to congratulate you and the nation, and to thank you for the perfect manner in which you entered into my views on the subject, and for the management of the blockade, about which I was most anxious. It will not be long ere you are instructed by the Government: the first express would arrive about four o'clock this morning, and I attempt a telegraph message, but it is cloudy. I beg you will send for anything you may want, to me, and it shall be sent instantly; and I beg to present my respects to Napoleon, and if I can render him any civility, I will consider it my duty, as well as in gratitude for Captain Elphinstone's report of the attention he received from him on the field of battle.

During the 25th of July, the concourse of people round the ship was greater than the day before, and the anxiety of the Frenchmen was considerably augmented by the confidence with which the newspapers spoke of the intention to remove Bonaparte to St Helena. In the afternoon, he walked above an hour on deck, frequently stood at the gangway, or opposite to the quarterdeck ports, for the purpose of giving the people an opportunity of seeing him, and, whenever he observed any well-dressed women, pulled his hat oft; and bowed to them. At dinner he conversed as usual, was inquisitive about the kinds of fish produced on the coast of England, and ate part of a turbot that was at table, with much relish. He then spoke of the character of the fishermen and boatmen on our coast, saying:

They are generally smugglers as well as fishermen; at one time a great many of them were in my pay, for the purpose of obtaining intelligence, bringing money over to France, and assisting prisoners of war to escape. They even offered, for a large sum of money, to seize the person of Louis, and deliver him into my hands; but as they could not guarantee the preservation of his life, I would not give my consent to the measure.

At three in the morning of the 26th of July, Captain Sartorius returned from London; having carried my despatch announcing Bonaparte's intention to embark in the *Bellerophon*, and brought with him orders for me to proceed to Plymouth Sound. We immediately got under weigh, accompanied by the *Myrmidon* and *Slaney*. While heaving the anchor up, Las Cases came upon deck, when I told him the ship was ordered to Plymouth, supposing, if he thought it requisite, he would acquaint his master. Soon after the ship was at sea, Madame Bertrand made her appearance, when she attacked me with some warmth for having neglected to acquaint Bonaparte with the orders I had received, and told me he was excessively offended. As she had once or twice before, when everything did not go exactly as she wished, held the same language, I determined to ascertain whether Bonaparte had expressed any dissatisfaction, and, if so, to come to an explanation with him, as, though I was inclined to treat him with every proper consideration, it never was my intention to be looked upon as responsible to him for my movements; I therefore told Las Cases what she had said, and requested he would ascertain whether Napoleon really had felt displeased. He immediately went into the cabin, and on his return assured me that there must have been some mistake, as nothing of the kind had taken place.

The ship's removal to the westward was by no means an agreeable event to the suite of my guest: they naturally reasoned, that, had it been the intention of the British Government to allow him to land in England, he would not have been removed further from the Metropolis. He, however, made no observations on the subject himself; still affecting to consider the reports in the newspapers as the surmises of the editors.

We had, during the forenoon of the 26th of July, to beat up from the Start to Plymouth Sound, against a strong northerly wind. Bonaparte remained upon deck the greater part of the day. When going into the Sound, I pointed out the Breakwater to him, and described the manner in which they were forming it. He said, it was a great national undertaking, and highly honourable to the country; enquired the estimated expense, and seemed surprised, when I told him it was expected to be finished for something less than a million sterling. He added, "I have expended a large sum of money on the port of Cherbourg, and in forming the Boyart Fort, to protect the anchorage at Isle d'Aix; but I fear now, those and many other of my improvements will be neglected, and allowed to go to ruin."

When the ship had anchored, I informed him I was going to wait on the Commander-in-chief, and requested to know if I could convey any message from him. He desired me to return his thanks to Lord Keith, for the kind intentions he had expressed towards him in his letters to me, and to say he was extremely anxious to see his Lordship, if it could be done with propriety. On delivering his message to Lord Keith, he answered, " I would wait upon him with much pleasure, but, to tell you the truth, I have as yet received no instructions as to the manner in which he is to be treated; and until I do receive these, I cannot well visit him." He then gave me some precautionary orders to prevent his escape, or any attempt to effect it. From which I give the extracts below.

Extract of an Order from Admiral Viscount Keith, GCB, to Captain Maitland, of HMS *Bellerophon*, dated Hamoaze, July 26, 1815.

In addition to the orders already received, you are to pay the strictest regard and attention to the directions contained in the enclosed extract of a letter from the Secretary of the Admiralty. If General Gourgaud has not already been taken out of the *Slaney*, you are to cause him to be removed immediately into the ship you command. I enclose, for your information, a copy of a general order that I have issued, forbidding communication with the ship you command; and it is my intention to order the *Liffey* and *Eurotas* to anchor near you, and to row guard.

Extract of a Letter from the Secretary of the Admiralty to Admiral Viscount Keith, GCB, dated 24th July, 1815, enclosed in the foregoing.

Referring your Lordship to Mr Croker's letter of the 1st instant, respecting Bonaparte, I am to signify their Lordships' directions to you, to give the most positive orders to Captain Maitland to prevent all communication whatever with the shore but through him, and by him through your Lordship; and on no account to permit any person whatsoever to go on board the ship, without your Lordship's permission given in writing for that purpose; which permission, for obvious reasons, will only be granted in such cases as the public service may require: and proper measures are to be taken to prevent boats and small craft from crowding near the *Bellerophon*.

Your Lordship will restrict the captains and commanders of your squadron from communicating, until further orders, with the *Bellerophon*.

There was also enclosed the following copy of a Memorandum, addressed to the respective Captains of HM Ships *Liffey* and *Eurotas*.

Ville de Paris, in Hamoaze,
26th July, 1815.

MEMO:

The *Liffey* and *Eurotas* are to take up an anchorage on each side of the

Bellerophon, at a convenient distance, and observe the following directions, as well for the purpose of preventing the escape of Bonaparte, or any of his suite, from that ship, as for restraining shore-boats and others from approaching too close to her, either from curiosity or any other motive.

A constant watch of an officer, a quarter-watch, and double sentinels, are to be kept by day, as well as a boat manned and armed alongside, in constant readiness, as a guard-boat: the same precaution is to be observed all night, with the exception, that one of the boats, in charge of a lieutenant, is to row guard, and to be relieved every hour.

No shore-boats, or others, are to be suffered, either by night or by day, to approach nearer the *Bellerophon* than one cable's length; and no boats are to be permitted to loiter about the ship, even at that distance, either from curiosity or any other motive: neither the captains of the *Liffey* or *Eurotas*, nor any other officer belonging to those or any other ships, are to go on board the *Bellerophon*, either to visit, or on any pretence whatever, without permission from me in writing.

Signed, KEITH, Admiral.

A Copy.
Keith, Admiral.
To the respective Captains of the Liffey and Eurotas.

When I returned on board, I found the frigates had taken their positions as directed in the last order, and their boats were endeavouring as much as possible to keep the shore-boats at the specified distance from the ship. I stated to Bonaparte what Lord Keith had said; to which he answered, "I am extremely anxious to see the Admiral, and therefore beg he will not stand upon ceremony: I shall be satisfied to be treated as a private person, until the British Government has determined in what light I am to be considered." He then complained of the two frigates being placed as guard-ships over him, "as if," said he, "I were not perfectly secure on board a British line-of-battle ship;" and added, "The guard-ships' boats have been firing musquetry all the evening, to keep the shore-boats at a distance: it disturbs and distresses me, and I shall be obliged to you to prevent it, if it lies in your power." I immediately sent to the Captains of the frigates, to put a stop to the firing.

On the 27th of July, I received a letter from the Secretary of the Admiralty, of which I give an extract:

Extract of a Letter from the Secretary of the Admiralty, addressed to Captain Maitland, of HMS *Bellerophon*, dated 25th July, 1815.

I have received and laid before my Lords Commissioners of the Admiralty, your letter of yesterday's date, reporting your arrival in the *Bellerophon* in Torbay, accompanied by the *Myrmidon*, having on board Napoleon Bonaparte and suite, and transmitting a copy of a letter you had addressed to Admiral Lord Keith, reporting your proceedings, under the various circumstances which occurred prior to his embarkation, of which their Lordships have been pleased to direct me to signify their approval.

I waited on Lord Keith in the morning, and carried with me Bonaparte's original letter to the Prince Regent, which General Gourgaud had refused to deliver to Captain Sartorius: finding that one of his own officers would not be allowed to proceed with it, he now consented to its being forwarded through the Admiral. I reported to his Lordship all the occurrences of the previous day; and that, in consequence of the frequent repetition in the newspapers of its being the intention of his Majesty's Government to send Bonaparte to St Helena, he, as well as the officers of his suite, had expressed much uneasiness. I also carried a message from him, stating his desire to see his Lordship, and that he would willingly waive all ceremony, and be considered as a private person. To which Lord Keith answered, "I shall now have no difficulty whatever, having received full instructions as to the manner in which he is to be treated: he is to be considered as a General Officer, and have the respect due to that rank paid him, and no more: you may therefore say I shall wait on him tomorrow forenoon." He then put into my hands the following additional orders.

Extract of a Letter from Admiral Viscount Keith, GCB, addressed to Captain Maitland, of HMS *Bellerophon*, dated Ville de Paris, Hamoaze, 27th July, 1815.

> I herewith transmit an extract of an order, containing certain directions relative to Bonaparte and his suite, and you are forthwith to carry the same into execution; sending on board the *Liffey* or *Myrmidon*, with directions similar to those that have been addressed to yourself, such of his suite as are to be withdrawn from the ship you command.

Extract of an Order from the Lords Commissioners of the Admiralty, to Admiral Viscount Keith, GCB, dated July 25th, 1815.

> That he should give immediate orders, that, upon the arrival of the *Bellerophon*, Napoleon Bonaparte should remain, until the Prince Regent's further pleasure shall be signified, on board of that, or such other ship of war as we shall appoint, and shall not be permitted on any account to come on

shore; or to hold communication with the shore, or with other vessels, either personally, or by writing. Not more than four or five persons of his suite (exclusive of menial servants) are to remain on board the same ship with himself: the remainder of his suite are to be kept under similar restraint, on board of other vessels of war. Napoleon Bonaparte is to be considered and addressed as a General Officer.

In consequence of those orders, several of the officers of inferior rank, and some of the servants, were sent to the frigates appointed to guard us.

In the afternoon Sir Richard and Lady Strachan, accompanied by Mrs Maitland, came alongside the ship. Bonaparte was walking the deck, and, when I told him my wife was in the boat, he went to the gangway, pulled off his hat, and asked her if she would not come up and visit him. She shook her head; and I informed him, that my orders were so positive, I could not even allow her to come on board. He answered, "C'est dur, ça." "That is very hard." And addressing himself to her, "Milord Keith est un peu trop sévère; n'est-ce pas, Madame?" "Lord Keith is a little too severe; is he not, Madam?" He then said to me, "Ma foi, son portrait ne la flatte pas; elle est encore plus jolie que lui." "I assure you her portrait is not flattering; she is handsomer than it is." I told him Sir Richard Strachan was in the boat with her, and that he was second in command of the Channel fleet: he bowed to him, and said, "He appears a very young man to hold so high a rank."

There were this day a great many boats round the ship, full of people, among which were a number of well-dressed females. He expressed himself in strong terms of admiration of the beauty of the English women, and was desirous of knowing which were the ladies,—"les dames comme il faut," as he termed it; as they were all so well dressed that he could not distinguish them.

In the evening a letter was sent to me by Lord Keith, of which I subjoin an extract:

Extract of a Letter from Admiral Viscount Keith, GCB, addressed to Captain Maitland of HMS *Bellerophon*, dated Ville de Paris, Hamoaze, 27th July, 1815.

From the representation you have made to me of the dissatisfaction expressed by Bonaparte, on observing by the newspapers that he was to be sent to St Helena; it will be necessary that you redouble your vigilance to prevent his escape; and you are therefore to station double sentinels, and resort to every other means that may be necessary for frustrating any such intention.

On the 28th of July, Lord Keith came on board, between eleven and

The scene in Plymouth Sound, August 1815 by John James Chalon. Curious sightseers try to catch a glimpse of Napoleon on HMS *Bellerophon*.

twelve o'clock, and was shown by me into the cabin, where Count Bertrand introduced him to Bonaparte. I immediately withdrew, and cannot therefore state what passed between them; but Lord Keith afterwards informed me, that Bonaparte had been very anxious to know whether the Government had come to any determination with regard to his disposal; of which his Lordship professed total ignorance.

After Lord Keith came out of the cabin, he remained some time with Bonaparte's suite, who were collected in the state room. Madame Bertrand drew him aside, and entered into conversation with him, saying what she had repeated to me a hundred times, that it would be the height of injustice to send them to St Helena, and endeavouring to persuade him to interfere in preventing her husband at least from going, should Napoleon be sent there.

During the whole of the 29th of July it rained incessantly, and nothing worth relating took place: the Frenchmen were deprived of their usual amusement of admiring the ladies, and being admired in return, not a boat having made its appearance. They often remarked, with the characteristic vivacity of their nation, that they were placed in the situation of Tantalus,—so many beauties in view, without the possibility of approaching them.

On Sunday, the 30th of July, the crowd of boats was greater than I ever remember to have seen at one time. I am certain I speak within bounds when I state, that upwards of a thousand were collected round the ship, in each of which, on an average, there were not fewer than eight people. The crush was so great, as to render it quite impossible for the guard-boats to keep them off;

though a boat belonging to one of the frigates made use of very violent means to effect it, frequently running against small boats, containing women, with such force as nearly to upset them, and alarming the ladies extremely. The French officers were very indignant at such rude proceedings, saying, "Is this your English liberty? Were such a thing to happen in France, the men would rise with one accord and throw that officer and his crew overboard."

After the ship's arrival in England, Bonaparte seldom left the cabin earlier than five o'clock in the afternoon; passing his time in walking up and down the after-cabin, reading a great deal, (the books that seemed to occupy his attention, when I had an opportunity of observing him, were, a Life of Washington, and a translation of Ossian's Poems) and often falling asleep on the sopha, having within these two or three years become very lethargic.

I this day informed him, that Lord Keith had received an intimation, that Sir Henry Bunbury, one of the Under Secretaries of State, was to arrive in the course of the day with the decision of the British Government as to his future disposal. He asked me many questions, but, although Lord Keith had acquainted me that Bonaparte was to go to St Helena, he had at the same time desired me not to communicate this information, and I was therefore obliged to evade his interrogatories as I best could.

In the newspapers of this day there appeared the lists of persons proscribed by the Government of France. Among the first class were the names of Bertrand, Savary, and Lallemand: the first treated it with derision, the two others appeared much alarmed, and often asked me if I thought it possible the British Government would deliver them up to Louis. I said, "Decidedly not; you have been received on board an English man of war, and it never can be the intention of the Ministers to deliver you over to punishment." They were not, however, satisfied by any means; and a French frigate, bearing the white flag, which lay in Hamoaze, was an object of much jealousy to them.

When I waited on Lord Keith, the morning of the 31st of July, he acquainted me that Sir Henry Bunbury had arrived, and was to accompany him on board at ten o'clock. He also showed me a notification of the decision of Government respecting Bonaparte, in which he was styled General throughout. It stated, that he was to be sent to St Helena, and to be permitted to take with him three of the higher class of those that had accompanied him from France, and twelve domestics, who were to be selected by himself, with the exception of Savary and Lallemand, who were not on any account to be permitted to go with him. I immediately returned on board, to be in readiness to receive Lord Keith and Sir Henry Bunbury; and informed Bonaparte, that he might expect them. He asked me if I knew what they were to communicate; and having then received his Lordship's sanction for doing so, I told him, I understood it was determined he was to be sent to St Helena. His mind had, by this time, been so much prepared by the newspapers for that event, that he did not show any very strong emotion at receiving the intimation; though he complained, in strong terms, of the injustice of such a measure. As, however, the Admiral's barge was seen approaching, and I was obliged to go upon deck to receive him, I had very little conversation with him at that time.

Lord Keith and Sir Henry Bunbury arrived about half-past ten in the forenoon, when I showed them into the cabin, where Bonaparte was attended by Count Bertrand. I then withdrew, leaving them shut up with him for about half an hour, when Lord Keith called me into the fore-cabin, where all the suite were assembled, and I presented each of them to the Admiral and Sir Henry. They all appeared very much distressed, but particularly Savary and Lallemand; who were extremely urgent to know how they were to be disposed of; protesting, most vehemently, against their being given up to France, as a breach of all faith and honour. Madame Bertrand again tried to induce Lord Keith to use his influence with our Government, to prevent Bertrand from accompanying Bonaparte to St Helena.

As soon as the Admiral had left the ship, Bonaparte sent for me, and showed me the same paper Lord Keith had communicated to me in the morning. When I had read it, he complained vehemently of his treatment in being sent to St Helena, saying, "The idea of it is perfect horror to me. To be placed for life on an island within the Tropics, at an immense distance from any land, cut off from all communication with the world, and everything that I hold dear in it!—c'est pis que la cage de fer de Tamerlan. (It is worse than Tamerlane's iron cage.) I would prefer being delivered up to the Bourbons. Among other insults," said he,—"but that is a mere bagatelle, a very secondary consideration,—they style me General! they can have no right to call me General; they may as well call me Archbishop, for I was head of the church, as well as the army. If they do not acknowledge me as Emperor, they ought as First Consul; they have sent Ambassadors to me as such; and your King, in his letters, styled me brother. Had they confined me in the Tower of London, or one of the fortresses in England, (though not what I had hoped from the generosity of the English people,) I should not have so much cause of complaint; but to banish me to an island within the Tropics! They might as well have signed my death-warrant at once, as it is impossible a man of my habit of body can live long in such a climate."

He then expressed a desire to write another letter to the Prince Regent; and I carried it the same afternoon to Lord Keith, by whom it was immediately forwarded to London.

Generals Savary and Lallemand this day made many appeals to me on the injustice of our Government delivering them up to France; saying they had not a doubt it was intended, else why except them from accompanying the

Emperor, as they were both married men, and Savary the father of a large family:—it was not the wish of either to have gone to St Helena; but their being expressly excepted, and their names appearing in the list of proscribed, was but too sure a proof of their intended fate. Savary added, "Were I to be allowed a fair and impartial trial, I should have nothing to fear, never having accepted a situation under Louis; but at present, when faction runs so high, I should inevitably be sacrificed to the fury of party. Lallemand's case is quite different: he held a command under the King, and, on Napoleon's return from Elba, joined him with his troops; therefore, his situation would at any time be a dangerous one:—but I lived in the country all the time Louis was in France, and did not come forward until Bonaparte's arrival in Paris, when he directed me to take the command of the Gendarmerie."

Lallemand said, "My reason for coming on board the *Bellerophon* with Las Cases on the morning of the 14th, was to ascertain whether there would be a risk of any of the Emperor's followers being delivered up to the French Government, in the event of their accompanying him to England; when you assured me there could be no danger of it." I replied, "My answer to you was, that I was of opinion there could be no risk of the British Government taking such a step; and I see no reason now to alter that opinion. As I have received you on board the *Bellerophon*, I consider you under the protection of the British flag, and myself, in a great measure, responsible for your personal safety; and under that impression I will write on the subject to Lord Melville, as the Minister under whose immediate control I act, that your minds may be set at rest, though, I repeat, you run no hazard of being sent to France." The same evening, before I went to bed, I wrote the letter which follows:—

HMS *Bellerophon*,
Plymouth Sound, 31st July, 1815.

My Lord,

I am induced to address your Lordship in consequence of having observed, in the intimation delivered to Napoleon Bonaparte of the number of persons allowed to accompany him to the Island of St Helena, that the names of Savary and Lallemand are expressly excepted, which, together with their being proscribed in the French newspapers, has created in them a belief that it is the intention of His Majesty's Government to deliver them up to the King of France. Far be it from me to assume such an idea; but I hope your Lordship will make allowance for the feelings of an officer who has nothing so dear to him as his honour, and who could not bear that a stain should be affixed to a name he has ever endeavoured to bear unblemished. These two

Napoleon on HMS *Bellerophon* at Plymouth. A portrait by Sir Charles Lock Eastlake, July-August 1815.

men, Savary and Lallemand (what their characters or conduct in their own country may be I know not), threw themselves under the protection of the British flag; that protection was granted them with the sanction of my name. It is true, no conditions were stipulated for; but I acted in the full confidence that their lives would be held sacred, or they should never have put foot in the ship I command, without being made acquainted that it was for the purpose of delivering them over to the laws of their country.

I again beg leave to repeat to your Lordship, that I am far from supposing it to be the intention of His Majesty's Government to deliver these men over to the laws of their country; but, as they are strongly impressed with that belief, and I look upon myself as the cause of their being in their present situation, I most earnestly beg your Lordship's influence may be exerted that two men may not be brought to the scaffold who claimed and obtained at my hands the protection of the British flag.

> I have the honour to be,
> &c. &c. &c.
> Fred. L. Maitland.

The Viscount Melville,
&c. &c. &c.

I felt convinced that Bonaparte, after the notification he had received, would be too much depressed in spirits to make his appearance on deck this day; and sent a boat to some of my friends, who were waiting in hopes of seeing him, to say there was no chance of his coming out, as he was much distressed at the communication which had been made to him: I was, therefore, a good deal surprised, on turning round, to find him standing at my elbow; and I can only account for his showing himself as usual, by supposing either that he was not in fact so much annoyed as I had believed him to be, or that he was actuated by a desire of creating a feeling of commiseration among the English people in his behalf.

At dinner he conversed as usual; and, indeed, it was quite astonishing with what elasticity his spirits regained their usual cheerfulness, after such trials and disappointments. He never, in my hearing, threatened to commit suicide; nor do I believe he did on any occasion: the only expression I ever heard him make use of, that could in any way be construed into such a threat, was, that he would not go to St Helena,—"Je n'irai pas à St Hélène."

As Bonaparte always retired early to bed, it was the custom for the French ladies and officers to assemble every evening in the ward-room, and partake of wine and water, punch, or bishop—a mixture consisting of Port, Madeira, nutmeg, and other ingredients, well known to sailors, and much relished by our foreign guests.

I was sitting this evening next Montholon, when Madame Bertrand entered; I said to her, "Will you not sit down and take something?" She gave an answer which I took for No; and passed rapidly into the first lieutenant's cabin, which she had occupied since she came on board. Montholon, who had observed her with more attention than I had done, immediately rose and followed her. There was instantly a shriek from the cabin, and a great uproar; and someone called out 'The Countess is overboard.' I ran upon deck, that, in the event of its being so, a boat might be lowered down, or the guard-boats called to her assistance. On looking over the quarter, and seeing no splash in the water, I felt satisfied it was a false alarm, and returned to the ward-room. Madame Bertrand had by this time been placed on her bed, where she was lying in strong hysterics, at intervals abusing the English nation and its Government, in the most vehement and unmeasured terms; sometimes in French and sometimes in English. Lallemand was walking up and down the ward-room much agitated, joining in the abuse; saying, among other things, "that it was horrible to bring a set of people on board the ship for the purpose of butchering them." I turned to him, and said, "Monsieur Lallemand, what a woman says in the state of violent irritation that Madame Bertrand at present is, I consider of little consequence, and am willing to make every allowance for the situation you are placed in; but I cannot stand by and hear such terms used of the Government of my country; and if you do not desist, or make use of more respectful language, I shall be under the necessity of taking measures that will be very unpleasant both to you and myself."

This had the effect of silencing him. When the bustle had subsided, I retired to my cabin, and was employed in writing the foregoing letter to Lord Melville, in behalf of Messrs Savary and Lallemand; when the latter, attended by Generals Montholon and Gourgaud, came in. They immediately entered into conversation with me about the cruelty of their situation: among many other things, they said, "You may depend upon it, the Emperor never will go to St Helena; he will sooner put himself to death; he is a man of determined character, and what he says he will do." "Has he ever said he will put himself to death?" I asked. They answered, "No; but he has said he will not go, which amounts to the same thing; and were he to consent himself, here are three of us who are determined to prevent him." I told them they had better consider the consequences well, before they ventured on a measure of that kind.

The next day, August 1st, 1815, I waited on Lord Keith, and reported all that had occurred during the preceding day. I also showed him the letter I had written and meant to send to Lord Melville, respecting Generals Savary and Lallemand; he read it, and said, "that though he did not agree with me in opinion as to my honour or character being implicated, yet that he saw no harm in the letter." He then said, "You may tell those gentlemen who have threatened to be Bonaparte's executioners, that the law of England awards death to murderers, and that the certain consequence of such an act will be finishing their career on a gallows."

After quitting his Lordship, I had an interview with Sir Henry Bunbury, previous to his setting out for London, and stated to him my feelings respecting the cruelty of delivering up to the French Government, men who had been received under the protection of the British flag. I said that I had no belief myself that any such intention existed; but that they were so strongly impressed with the conviction of it, that I had been induced to write to Lord Melville, and now begged to state to him, that I should consider myself dishonoured for ever, if they suffered death through my means. He listened, but did not speak till I had finished; when he told me he would repeat what I had said to his Majesty's Ministers.

Madame Bertrand kept her bed the whole of this day, and did not appear at dinner. When Bonaparte came upon deck, he asked Mr O'Meara, the surgeon, after her health; and then said, with an incredulous smile, "Do you really think, Doctor, she meant to drown herself?" I put the same question to Montholon; who said he had not a doubt of it, for, when he followed her into the cabin, she was in the act of throwing herself out of the gallery window; that he rushed forward and caught hold of her, and that she continued suspended by the bar that goes across the window, with the greater part of her body hanging out, until he received assistance to drag her in. The bar above-mentioned had been placed there for the purpose of preventing people from falling overboard when the window was open and the ship had much motion at sea.

On returning on board after being with Lord Keith, I went into Madame Bertrand's cabin to see how she was, and found her in bed. I asked her, how she could be so indiscreet as to attempt to destroy herself? "Oh! I am driven to desperation," she said; "I do not know what I do; I cannot persuade my husband to remain behind, he being determined to accompany the Emperor to St Helena." She then ran into a great deal of abuse of Napoleon, saying, "If his ends are served, he does not care what becomes of other people. 'Tis true he has always given Bertrand lucrative and honourable situations, but the expense attending them is such, that it was impossible to save money; and he has never given him a grant of land, or anything that permanently bettered our fortune." On another occasion, she came into the cabin which I occupied, when I was writing, and, after exacting a promise of secrecy towards the remainder of the suite, she entreated I would take measures to prevent her husband from accompanying Bonaparte, and begged me to write a letter in her name to Lord Keith, to induce him to interfere. I told her it would appear extremely officious in me to write on such a subject, but that anything she chose to put on paper I would deliver to his Lordship. She did write, and I carried the letter; but his Lordship declined interfering, desiring me to say, he considered it the duty of every good wife to follow the fortunes of her husband. In the course of the conversation above-mentioned, she became extremely warm in speaking of Napoleon, saying, "He deserves nothing at our hands; and, indeed, there is not one of his people who would not most gladly quit him." Whenever she became animated, she could not pour out her feelings in the English language fast enough, (though she spoke it remarkably well, having received her education partly in England,) when she had always recourse to French; and though I frequently reminded her that there was nothing but a piece of canvas between us and the ward-room, where there were generally some of the French officers, I could by no means keep her within bounds. The consequence of which was, that all she said was heard and understood by one of them. When Madame Bertrand had left me, Count Montholon requested to speak with me in private. He carried me up to his cabin on the quarter-deck, where I found Generals Gourgaud and Lallemand, who told me they had been informed of what Madame Bertrand had said to me; and they had requested to see me, for the purpose of contradicting her assertion, that they were desirous of quitting Bonaparte: that, so far from that being the case, there was not one of them that would not follow him with pleasure wherever he might be sent, or that would not lay down his life to serve him: they also required secrecy towards

George Keith Elphinstone, 1st Viscount Keith GCB (1746-1823). A portrait by George Sanders.

On the renewal of the war in 1803 Keith was appointed commander-in-chief in the North Sea, which post he held till 1807. In February 1812 he was appointed commander-in-chief in the English Channel, and in 1814 he was raised to a viscounty. During his last two commands he was engaged first in overlooking the measures taken to meet a threatened invasion. He was at Plymouth when Napoleon surrendered and was brought to England in HMS *Bellerophon.* The decisions of the British Government were expressed through him to the fallen Emperor. Lord Keith refused to be led into disputes, and confined himself to declaring steadily that he had his orders to obey.

the Countess. I answered, "Why really, gentlemen, this is very extraordinary; you pretend to know all that passed in a private conversation I have had with Madame Bertrand, and then to bind me to secrecy: you may depend upon it, I will enter into no such engagement, until I know by what means you obtained your information." They then told me that one of them had been in the quarter-gallery, and overheard all she said.

Nothing of importance occurred during the 2nd of August. Bonaparte did not appear upon deck; nor would he consent to nominate the people who were to accompany him to St Helena; he still seemed to indulge a hope, that the Government might be induced to reconsider the decision. I had half an hour's conversation with him in the cabin: it consisted, on his part, of complaints of the cruelty of sending him to St Helena. He likewise asked me many questions about that island, as to its extent, climate, and productions, whether it would be possible to take exercise on horseback, if there was game of any kind upon it, &c. to all of which I could only answer from report, never having visited the island myself. He conversed very little at dinner, and appeared unwell. In the evening, General Bertrand informed me that the sentinel's calling out "All's well!" during the night disturbed him, and prevented his sleeping; upon which I gave directions they should not do so while he remained on board.

During the 3rd of August Bonaparte kept his cabin. When I went to the Admiral, I met him escorting some ladies, in company with Sir William Lemon, to the *Ville de Paris's* barge. On being introduced to Sir William, he told me that a report was in circulation that a boat was to have been under the *Bellerophon*'s stern the night before, at ten o'clock, for the purpose of effecting Bonaparte's escape. Although I gave no credit to the report, I immediately returned on board, and asked the first lieutenant if Bonaparte had been seen that morning; he informed me that he had not attended breakfast, and that no person had seen him but his own people. I then sent to the *Eurotas*, which lay astern of the ship, to enquire if he had appeared at the stern windows; but was answered in the negative: upon which I desired one of the young gentlemen to go out on the spanker-boom and look into the cabin windows, to ascertain if he was sitting on the sofa; but he could not discover him in any part of the cabin. I then became extremely uneasy, and sent my servant in to bring some paper out, who on entering found the object of my anxiety stretched out on his bed with his clothes on, and the curtains drawn close round him, with every appearance of being unwell. I had before asked Count Bertrand about him, who said he had passed a bad night, and was too ill to leave his apartment.

Instead of retiring to his bed this evening between eight and nine o'clock, as was his usual custom, I heard him and another person (I believe General Bertrand) pacing up and down the cabin until past eleven; and in consequence gave directions to the officer of the watch and the sentries to be particularly vigilant; and ordered one of the guard-boats to remain under the ship's stern all night. He had still declined all this day giving a list of those that he wished to attend him to St Helena.

At three in the morning of the 4th of August, the officer of the watch brought me a letter from Lord Keith, informing me that a courier had just arrived from London, and that it was probable the ship would be required to put to sea at a moment's notice. In consequence of this order, we unmoored at daylight, bent the top-gallant sails, and made other preparations for getting under weigh. The Frenchmen were very watchful of all our motions, appeared much alarmed and annoyed, and questioned me frequently as to the cause. I told them, what was literally the fact, that I had received directions to be ready to put to sea, but had no orders to carry it into effect; and that was all I knew.

Between seven and eight o'clock, I waited on Lord Keith, who said he had received information that a habeas corpus had been taken out for the purpose of bringing Bonaparte on shore, and that a lawyer was on his way down to serve it; desiring me, therefore, to be ready to put to sea whenever the signal might be made.

On returning on board, I had an interview with Bonaparte, who was very urgent to know why the ship was preparing for sea. I told him, by Lord Keith's directions, that it was the intention of our Government, his removal should take place at sea; and that we were going out to meet the *Northumberland*, the ship which was to convey him to St Helena.

He begged I would write to Lord Keith, and say he wished very much to see him; and Count Bertrand told me he was also desirous of having the newspapers. I accordingly wrote to his Lordship, who was then on board the *Tonnant*: who, however, declined visiting him, but sent me a note, of which the following is an extract.

Extract of a Note from Admiral Viscount Keith, addressed to Captain Maitland, of HMS *Bellerophon*, dated *Tonnant*, 4th August.

> I send you the paper, and shall be glad to hear the determination of the General, whom you may inform that the answer is arrived from London, and that I have no authority to alter, in any degree, any part of the former communication; which induces me to wish the selection of the persons he is inclined should attend him.

I communicated the contents to General Bertrand, who made his report to Bonaparte. On his coming out of the cabin, I pressed him on the subject of nominating those that were to go with him to St Helena; but the only answer he returned was, "L'Empereur n'ira pas à St Hélène;"—"the Emperor will not go to St Helena."

Soon after nine o'clock, the *Bellerophon*'s signal was made to prepare to weigh, and at half-past nine to weigh: we immediately started. As the light air of wind that blew was right into the Sound, and the flood-tide against us, the guard-boats were sent ahead to tow; but, soon observing a suspicious-looking person in a boat approaching the ship, I ordered one of them to cast off, keep under the ship's stern, and not allow any shore boat, under any pretext, to come near us. The person alluded to proved afterwards to have been the lawyer mentioned by Lord Keith; not with a Habeas Corpus, but a subpœna for Bonaparte to attend a trial at the Court of King's Bench as a witness. He was, however, foiled: as Lord Keith avoided him, and got on board the *Prometheus*, off the Ramehead, where he remained until joined by the *Tonnant*; while the guard-boat prevented him from approaching near enough to the *Bellerophon*, to serve his writ on me.

To prevent erroneous impressions from going abroad, and to put this curious circumstance in its true light, I have prevailed on a friend, who was educated for the English bar, to favour me with the following account of the writs of the Habeas Corpus and subpœna; by which it will appear that no such process, or any other, as far as I can understand, could have had the effect of removing Bonaparte from one of His Majesty's ships, and musing him to be landed in England in opposition to the commands of the Government of the country.

It is a common mistake to suppose that the celebrated Habeas Corpus Act made it a matter of right, for every person, under any restraint whatever to obtain this writ. That statute related to persons committed by legal process for criminal offences, and the object of it was to prevent them being detained an unnecessary or unreasonable length of time, without being brought to trial. Other cases of alleged illegal detention were left as at common law: in these the granting or refusal of the writ is discretionary in the Court, or Judge applied to, and it will only be issued on a proper case being laid before them. No such writ, it is believed, was ever applied for in Bonaparte's case; nor, if applied for, would it have been obtained. Where a foreigner, in private life, is brought to England, and detained against his will, the Court will grant the writ; but any application of Bonaparte, or on his behalf, must have shown him to have surrendered, and to have been then detained as a prisoner of war. Under that character, he was not entitled to the benefit of this writ; the Courts having refused it on the application of individuals brought to England as prisoners of war, even when applied for by the subject of a neutral power, who swore to his having been compelled by force to serve the enemy, and to have been captured in the course of that compulsory service.

The real transaction alluded to, is understood to have been this: an individual being under prosecution for a libel on a naval officer, censuring his conduct on the West India station, when a French squadron was in those seas, pretended that it would aid his defence to show that the French ships were at that time in an unserviceable condition, and that Bonaparte would be able to prove the fact. He accordingly obtained a subpœna for him to attend as a witness on the trial in the Court of King's Bench, and endeavoured himself, and not by a lawyer, as at first supposed, to get on board the *Bellerophon* to deliver it.

This transaction probably gave currency to the rumours of a Habeas Corpus having been issued, particularly as one description of that writ is, the proceeding for bringing a prisoner into Court to give evidence, which having given, he is remanded to gaol.

Had the individual in question succeeded in his attempt to get on board the ship, and deliver the subpœna, it would have been of no assistance either to himself or Bonaparte, if it was at all intended to benefit the latter, as it would not have been possible for him to obey it, there not being any authority for Captain Maitland, who was answerable for his safety as a prisoner, allowing him to do so. It was, however, considered the most prudent course, by Lord Keith, not to permit the delivery of the process, the exact nature of which was at the moment unknown, lest it might involve himself or Captain Maitland in any difficulty, by an apparent disrespect to the Court, and more particularly as it might create erroneous impressions in Bonaparte's mind, that a breach of the law was committed in his not being permitted to comply with the terms of the document, not aware that it contained no power authorising his release from detention as a prisoner of war.

While the ship was working out of the Sound, two well-dressed women in a boat kept as close to her as the guard-boat would allow, and, whenever Bonaparte appeared at the stern windows, stood up and waved their handkerchiefs.

On joining the *Prometheus* off the Ramehead, where Lord Keith's flag was then flying, I received the following note from his Lordship.

No date; received August 4th, in the Afternoon.
I have been chased all day by a lawyer with a Habeas Corpus: he is landed at Cawsand, and may come off in a sailing-boat during the night; of course, keep all sorts of boats off, as I will do the like in whatever ship I may be in.

KEITH.

Captain Maitland.

Bonaparte wrote another letter this evening to the Prince Regent, which I carried to Lord Keith, who again told me of his having been chased all day by a lawyer: who had first started him out of his own house, then followed him to the *Tonnant*, where he attempted to get in at one side, as his Lordship left her on the other; he afterwards pursued him towards Cawsand, but the Admiral being in a twelve-oared barge, out-rowed him, and gave him the slip round the Ramehead. It was on his return from this chase that he attempted to get on board the *Bellerophon*.

Bonaparte now confined himself entirely to his cabin, never coming on deck, or appearing at breakfast or dinner. He was not served from the table, but what he ate was prepared and carried in to him by Marchand, his favourite valet de chambre. Messrs Bertrand and Las Cases passed much time with him; and this evening the protest was prepared, which will appear in the sequel.

On the morning of the 5th of August, the weather was overcast, with a strong breeze of wind, and the sea began to rise, much to the discomposure of my poor French guests. Soon after breakfast, my signal being made from the *Tonnant*, where Lord Keith had now hoisted his flag, I told General Bertrand that I was going to the Admiral, and would convey anything Bonaparte had to say to him. He requested I would wait until a letter or paper, then under preparation, was finished, which was intended for me, but a copy to be presented to Lord Keith. I waited nearly an hour, when he brought me Bonaparte's protest. I delivered it to the Admiral, stating at the same time that I wished to have a copy; and was afterwards furnished with one by his Lordship's secretary. I insert it here.

Bonaparte's Protest

Je proteste solennellement ici, à la face du Ciel et des hommes, contre la violence qui m'est faite, contre la violation de mes droits les plus sacrés, en disposant par la force, de ma personne et de ma liberté.

Je suis venu librement à bord du *Bellerophon*; je ne suis point prisonnier; je suis l'hôte de l'Angleterre. J'y suis venu à l'instigation même du Capitaine qui a dit avoir des ordres du Gouvernement de me recevoir, et de me conduire en Angleterre avec ma suite, si cela m'étoit agreable. Je me suis présenté de bonne foi pour venir me mettre sous la protection des loix d'Angleterre. Aussitôt asais à bord du *Bellerophon*, je fus sur le foyer du peuple Britannique. Si le Gouvernement, en donnant des ordres au Capitaine du *Bellerophon*, de me recevoir ainsi que ma suite, n'a voulu que tendre une embûche, il a forfait à l'honneur et flêtri son pavillon. Si cet acte se consommoit, ce seroit en vain que les Anglais voudroient parler à l'Europe de leur loyauté, de leur loix, et de leur liberté. La foi Britannique *s'y trouvera perdue dans l'hospitalité du Bellerophon*. J'en appelle à l'histoire; elle dira qu'un ennemi qui fit vingt ans la guerre aux peuples Anglois, vint librement, dans son infortune, chercher un asile sous ses loix. Quelle plus éclatante preuve pouvait-il lui donner de son estime et de sa confiance? Mais comment réponditon en Angleterre à une telle magnanimité?—On feignit de tendre une main hospitalière à cet ennemi, et quand il se fut livré de bonne foi, on l'immola.

Signé, NAPOLÉON.
À bord du *Bellerophon*,
4 Aout, 1815.

Translation

Bonaparte's Protest

I hereby solemnly protest, in the face of Heaven and of men, against the violence done me, and against the violation of my most sacred rights, in forcibly disposing of my person and my liberty. I came voluntarily on board of the *Bellerophon*; I am not a prisoner, I am the guest of England. I came on board even at the instigation of the Captain, who told me he had orders from the Government to receive me and my suite, and conduct me to England, if agreeable to me. I presented myself with good faith to put myself under the protection of the English laws. As soon as I was on board the *Bellerophon*, I was under shelter of the British people.

If the Government, in giving orders to the Captain of the *Bellerophon* to receive me as well as my suite, only intended to lay a snare for me, it has forfeited its honour and disgraced its flag.

If this act be consummated, the English will in vain boast to Europe of their integrity, their laws, and their liberty. British good faith will be lost in the hospitality of the *Bellerophon.*

I appeal to History; it will say that an enemy, who for twenty years waged war against the English people, came voluntarily, in his misfortunes, to seek an asylum under their laws. What more brilliant proof could he give of his esteem and his confidence? But what return did England make for so much magnanimity? They feigned to stretch forth a friendly hand to that enemy; and when he delivered himself up in good faith, they sacrificed him.

Signed, NAPOLEON.
On board the *Bellerophon*,
4th August 1815.

On the above I shall only observe, that no snare had been laid, either on the part of His Majesty's Government or mine. I was placed before Rochefort for the open purpose of preventing Bonaparte from making his escape from that port; and the exertions of myself and those under my command had been so completely successful, that the intention of forcing past the ships under my orders, as well as every other plan proposed, of which there appear to have been several, were abandoned as utterly hopeless. And so far was I from seeking communication with Napoleon, that all the flags of truce proceeding from him, were strongly reprobated by me, as improper, except in extra-ordinary cases, and were only resorted to when, as appears from Lord Keith's letter of the 23rd of July, orders had been sent from Paris for his arrest, and when (as has since been proved) one or more intimations had been given by the officer commanding in Isle d'Aix, that, if he did not depart, he would be under the necessity of detaining him. Besides, it is now perfectly ascertained, that the determination of repairing to England was adopted at a consultation held by Bonaparte on the night of the 13th of July, when his letter to the Prince Regent was written; and Messrs Las Cases and Lallemand were sent on the morning of the 14th to discover if I would receive him on board the *Bellerophon*, and convey him to that country.

On the morning of the 6th of August, when walking the deck with Monsieur Las Cases, he for the first time mentioned, that he understood me to have assured him that the Emperor would be well received in England, and allowed to reside there. I replied, "I cannot conceive how you could so far misunderstand me, as I constantly, in my communications with you, stated that I could make no promises whatever: that I thought my orders would bear me out in receiving him on board, and conveying him to England; but even in doing that, I acted very much upon my own responsibility. You questioned me frequently, as to my private opinion; and as I was quite ignorant upon the subject, I could only say I had no reason to believe he would be ill received." It did not, however, require my assistance to raise the hopes of those about Bonaparte, respecting the manner in which he was to be received in England; as one of his followers, on the passage home, asked me if I thought the Prince Regent would confer the order of the Garter upon him. If there was any misunderstanding, (which I cannot allow to have been the case,) Monsieur Las Cases has himself to blame. When he came on board of the *Bellerophon* for the purpose of treating, he concealed his knowledge of the English language; which, as I had considerable difficulty in expressing myself in French, could only be intended for the purpose of throwing me off my guard, that he might take advantage of any expressions that fell from me, or the officers I had always present at our meetings. Even after he was on board with Bonaparte, though he acknowledged he could read English, and always translated the newspapers for his master, he affected not to be able to speak it. What his actual knowledge of the language was, the following extract of a letter, from a friend of mine on board the *Northumberland*, dated—at sea, August the 22nd, 1815, will show:

> I do not know, whether Las Cases ever let you know he could speak English; but this I can assure you, that he speaks it very near as well as Madame Bertrand, and can hold a conversation, or maintain an argument in it, with as much fluency as she can.

This forenoon, I had a long conversation with Bonaparte. He complained bitterly of the conduct of the British Government; and entered, at considerable length, into the state of his affairs when he determined upon the measure of repairing on board the *Bellerophon*. "There still," said he, "was a large party in the South, that wished me to put myself at its head; the army behind the Loire was also desirous of my return. At ten o'clock of the night before I embarked, a deputation from the garrison of Rochelle waited upon me, with an offer to conduct me to the army; in addition to which, the troops that were in Rochefort, Bordeaux, and Isle d'Aix, amounting to twelve thousand men, were at my disposal. But I saw there was no prospect of ultimate success, though I might have occasioned a great deal of trouble and bloodshed, which I did not choose should take place on my account individually;—while the Empire was at stake, it was another matter."

In the afternoon, Mr O'Meara, the surgeon, informed me that General Savary had made a proposal to him to accompany Bonaparte to St Helena as

Barry Edward O'Meara, (1782-1836); Medical Attendant to Napoleon until 25 July 1818 when Sir Hudson Lowe, the Governor at St Helena caused him to be removed.

his medical attendant; Monsieur Maingaut, his surgeon, being a young man with whom he was little acquainted, having suffered so much from seasickness in the passage from Rochefort, that he felt averse to undertaking another sea voyage. He consulted me as to the propriety of accepting the offer. I told him it must depend very much upon his own feelings; but if he had no dislike to it, he had better accept the proposal, on condition that our Government consented, and agreed to pay his salary; but, in that case, an official communication must pass, through me, to the Admiral on the subject. This was the first intimation I received of Bonaparte having made any arrangement towards complying with the notification he had received from our Government.

About nine a.m. a large ship was seen to leeward, which, on closing, proved to be the *Northumberland*. The whole squadron then stood in, and anchored to the westward of Berryhead. I went on board the *Tonnant*, and reported to Lord Keith that Bonaparte had at last made up his mind to move from the *Bellerophon* without force being used; and that Count Bertrand was desirous of seeing his Lordship, that he might make the necessary arrangements about the people who were to accompany him. By the Admiral's directions, I returned to my ship and brought Monsieur Bertrand to him. Soon after Sir George Cockburn arrived, and they were shut up together for nearly two hours.

When I first went on board the *Tonnant*, I received a memorandum from Lord Keith, from which I give an extract; and at the same time a verbal intimation, that I should receive an order in writing the next day, to remove Bonaparte, and such part of his suite as he might select, to the *Northumberland*.

General Henri Gratien Comte de Bertrand, (1773-1844). Count Bertrand remained with Napoleon throughout the captivity. In 1840 he was chosen by the French Government, following agreement with the British Government to bring Napoleon's remains to France — *le retour des cendres.*

Extract of a Memorandum from Admiral Viscount Keith, GCB, addressed to Captain Maitland, of HMS *Bellerophon*, dated *Tonnant*, off the Start, 6th August, 1815.

> All arms of every description are to be taken from the Frenchmen of all ranks on board the ship you command; and they are to be carefully packed up and kept in your charge, while they remain on board the *Bellerophon*; and afterwards in that of the captain of the ship to which they may be removed.

While we were at dinner, Generals Bertrand and Montholon were employed making out lists of what would be required by the French officers and the ladies, to render them comfortable during their voyage to St Helena, which were despatched to Plymouth by Sir George Cockburn's secretary.

In the course of the evening Lord Keith and Sir George Cockburn came on board the *Bellerophon*; when the latter was introduced to Bonaparte.

As soon as General Bertrand was at leisure, I told him I had orders to remove Napoleon to the *Northumberland* the following day, and also to take away the arms from him and his attendants, giving him to understand that they would be returned on their arrival at their destination. He seemed much hurt at being deprived of his arms, but said he would give directions for their being delivered; and I received them the next morning, with the exception of Bonaparte's sword, which, by an order I subsequently received from Lord Keith, he was permitted to wear, when quitting the ship.

About half-past nine in the evening, Mons. Bertrand told me that Bonaparte was desirous of seeing me. On going into his cabin, he said, "Bertrand informs me you have received orders to remove me to the *Northumberland*; is it so?" I answered in the affirmative. "Have you any objection," he said, "to writing a letter to Bertrand, acquainting him of it; that I may have a document to prove that I was forced to quit the ship, and that my inclinations were not consulted." I replied, "I can have no objection to write such a letter, and shall do it this evening." I was then going to retire, when he requested me to remain, having more to say. "Your Government," he continued, "has treated me with much severity, and in a very different way from what I had hoped and expected, from the opinion I had formed of the character of your countrymen. It is true I have always been the enemy of England, but it has ever been an open and declared one; and I paid it the highest compliment it was possible for man to do in throwing myself on the generosity of your Prince: I have not now to learn, however, that it is not fair to judge of the character of a people by the conduct of their Government." He then went on, (alluding to the Government,) "They say I made no conditions. Certainly I made no conditions; how could an individual enter into terms with a nation? I wanted nothing of them but hospitality, or, as the ancients would express it, 'air and water.' My only wish was to purchase a small property in England, and end my life there in peace and tranquillity. As for you, Capitaine," (the name by which he always addressed me) "I have no cause of complaint; your conduct to me has been that of a man of honour; but I cannot help feeling the severity of my fate, in having the prospect of passing the remainder of my life on a desert island. But," added he with a strong emphasis, "if your Government give up Savary and Lallemand to the King of France, they will inflict a stain upon the British name that no time can efface." I told him, in that respect, they were under an erroneous impression; that I was convinced it was not the intention of his Majesty's Ministers to deliver them up. "Je l'espère," "I hope so;" was his only reply.— I then took my leave of him for the night.

That I may not break in upon the occurrences of the 7th, I shall here insert the letter I wrote at Bonaparte's request, and a copy of the orders under which I acted in removing him from the *Bellerophon* to the *Northumberland*.

HMS *Bellerophon*, Start Bay,
7th August, 1815.

SIR,

I beg to acquaint you that I have this day received orders from Lord Keith, Commander in Chief of the Channel Fleet, to remove General Bonaparte from the ship I command, to his Majesty's ship *Northumberland*; and I have to request you will intimate the above to the General, that he may prepare for the removal.

I likewise enclose a copy of an order respecting the arms of General Bonaparte and the whole of his attendants, and request you will give directions for their being delivered to me, that they may be disposed of as the order directs.

I have the honour to be, &c. &c. &c.
Fred. L. Maitland.

Lieut. General Count Bertrand.
Copy of the order alluded to.
By the Right Hon. Viscount Keith, GCB, &c. &c. &c.

You are hereby required and directed to deliver the persons, named below, into the charge of Rear Admiral Sir George Cockburn.

Given on board the *Tonnant*, At anchor under Berryhead, 7th August, 1815.
KEITH, Admiral.

By command of the Admiral,
James Meek, Secretary.

To F. L. Maitland, Esq. Captain of HMS *Bellerophon*.

> General Bonaparte.
> Count Bertrand, his Wife, three children, one female servant, and her child.
> General Montholon, his Wife, one child, and one female servant.
> General Gourgaud.
> Le Comte de Las Cases, and his son.
> Marchand, Premier Valet de Chambre.
> St Denis, ditto.
> Novarra, ditto.
> Piéron, Chef d'Office.
> Le Page, Cuisinier.
> Archambaud, Premier Valet de Pied.
> Gentilini, Valet de Pied.
> Bernard, domestique du Comte Bertrand.

The four domestics underneath, who had come to England in the *Myrmidon*, also accompanied him:

Charles Tristan Comte de Montholon, (1783-1853). Count Montholon remained with Napoleon throughout the captivity.

Cipriani, Maître d'Hôtel.

Santini, Huissier.

Rousseau, Lampiste.

Archambaud, Valet de Pied.

Extract of a Letter from Admiral Viscount Keith, GCB, addressed to Captain Maitland, of HMS *Bellerophon*, dated *Tonnant*, off Berryhead, 7th August, 1815.

> When the General quits the ship, it is not intended to take his sword from him, but to let him wear it, but not the others. Pistols, guns, &c. must, as in all instances, be removed for the safety of the ship, but the arms are carefully to be kept, and restored at a proper occasion.

On the morning of the 7th of August, 1815, Count Las Cases made an application to me for permission to wait on Lord Keith, having a communication to make to him. I, in consequence, went to his Lordship, and obtained leave to send him. When the Admiral came on board the *Bellerophon*, in the forenoon, to attend Bonaparte in his removal to the *Northumberland*, he informed me that Monsieur Las Cases had represented to him, that I had promised Bonaparte should be well received in England, and allowed to remain there; and the same day he wrote a letter to me containing the above statement, and directing me to report upon it, which I afterwards did, as will hereafter appear.

Count Bertrand was employed, during the morning, making out a list of those that were to proceed to St Helena with Bonaparte, in which General Gourgaud's name was omitted, and Colonel Planat was nominated his Secretary. This offended Monsieur Gourgaud so much, that he made use of some very strong language to General Bertrand; and after a good deal of altercation, it was arranged, I believe by Bonaparte himself, that Gourgaud should take Planat's place. There was also another cause of disagreement. The number of domestics allowed to go to St Helena being only twelve, did not admit of all the officers taking their personal attendants; General Montholon was obliged to leave a servant who had been with him many years, and Count Bertrand's was the only exception.

General Bertrand had been so much employed all the morning making preparations for their removal, that he did not come to breakfast until everyone had finished; his wife remained at the table, as I did also, as a mark of attention to him. She soon commenced an attack on her husband, to induce him to quit Bonaparte and remain in England. He seemed much distressed, but remained silent. At last, she turned to me, and begged I would give an opinion, and use my influence in favour of her proposal. I said, "Madame Bertrand, I have from the beginning endeavoured to avoid meddling in the very unpleasant discussions that have been going on for some days; but, as you demand my opinion, and force me to give it, I must acquaint you that I think, if your husband quits his master at such a time as the present, he will forfeit the very high character he now bears in this country." I then rose from the table and went upon deck.

A short time after, Madame Bertrand came on deck, and, addressing me with much indignation in her countenance, said, "So, Captain Maitland, I hear the Emperor is not to have the whole of the after-cabin on board the *Northumberland*." I told her, I understood that Sir George Cockburn had received orders to that effect. "They had better treat him like a dog at once," said she, "and put him down in the hold." I had for several days been kept in a state of irritation that cannot be described, and such as few people have had an opportunity of experiencing. Madame Bertrand had, it will be readily understood, some share in causing this; and on her making the above remark, I am sorry to say, the little self-possession that still remained gave way, and I answered in these words, "Madam, you talk like a very foolish woman; and if you cannot speak more to the purpose, or with more respect of the Government I have the honour to serve, I request you will not address yourself to me." Just before she went out of the ship, however, she came up to me in a conciliatory and friendly manner, that did her the highest honour, and said, "Captain Maitland, you called me a very foolish woman this morning, but I should be sorry to part with you on bad terms; have you any objection

Louis Marchand, (1792-1876).
Marchand was First Valet to Napoleon
at Longwood and executor to his will.
His mother was nurse to Napoleon's
son, the King of Rome. He remained
throughout the captivity and returned
in 1840 for the exhumation and *le
retour des cendres*.

to shake hands with me? as God knows if we shall ever meet again." "Very far
from it," I answered; "I should be extremely sorry you left the ship without
receiving my good wishes for your happiness and prosperity; and if, in the
warmth of my temper, and under the harassing circumstances of my situation,
I have said anything unpleasant, I most sincerely beg your pardon, and hope
you will forgive and forget it."

Soon after, Sir George Cockburn came on board, attended by Mr Byng
as his secretary, for the purpose of examining Bonaparte's baggage: he
had directions to apply to some person of his suite to attend at the search.
The proposal was made to Count Bertrand; but he was so indignant at the
measure, that he positively refused either to be present himself or to direct
any other person to superintend. General Savary, however, consented, and
was present, as well as Marchand. The covers of the trunks were merely
opened, and Mr Byng passed his hand down the side, but the things were
not unpacked. Once or twice, when the door of the after-cabin was opened,
Bonaparte expressed his obligation to Mr Byng for the delicate manner
in which he conducted the search, by bowing to him. When they came to
the boxes containing the money, of which there were two, Marchand was
permitted to take out such sum as was considered necessary for paying the
wages of the servants that were to be left behind, and for other contingent
expenses. One box, containing four thousand gold Napoleons, was retained
and put under my charge, where it remained until my arrival in London,

when I delivered it to Sir Hudson Lowe to be restored to its owner, as will be seen by the following order, receipts, &c.

By the Right Hon. Viscount Keith, GCB, &c. &c. &c.

You are hereby required and directed to receive into your custody such a sum of money belonging to General Bonaparte, as will be delivered into your charge by Rear-Admiral Sir George Cockburn, granting proper receipts for the same.

Given on board the *Tonnant*, At anchor under Berryhead, 7th August, 1815.

KEITH, Admiral.

To F. L. Maitland, Esq. Captain of HMS *Bellerophon*.

J'ai laissé le sept d'aout, à bord du Bellerophon, à Monsieur le Capitaine Maitland, une somme de quatre vingt mille francs, en quatre mille Napoleons d'or.

MARCHAND,
Premier Valet de Chambre.

On the 7th of August, I have left on board the Bellerophon, in charge of Captain Maitland, the sum of eighty thousand francs, in four thousand gold Napoleons.

MARCHAND,
lst Valet de Chambre.

I acknowledge to have received a box with four paper packages, *said* to contain four thousand gold Napoleons, the property of Napoleon Bonaparte.

August 7th, 1815,

FRED. L. MAITLAND.
Approved, George Cockburn

As I shall not have to revert to the subject of the money, I shall here subjoin the receipt I obtained on delivering it at the Admiralty Office, though it is of a date some time posterior.

Admiral Sir George Cockburn, (1772-1853). As a captain he was present at the battle of Cape St Vincent in 1797. He later commanded the naval support at the reduction of Martinique in 1809.

He directed the capture and burning of Washington on 24 August 1814 as an advisor to Major General Robert Ross during the War of 1812.

He went on to be First Naval Lord and in that capacity sought to improve the standards of gunnery in the fleet, forming a gunnery school at Portsmouth; later he ensured that the Navy had latest steam and screw technology and put emphasis of the ability to manage seamen without the need to resort to physical punishment.

Frtom August to October 1815 he escorted Napoleon to St Helena on board HMS *Northumberland*.

A portrait by John James Halls, *c.* 1817 showing the burning of Washington as a background.

Admiralty, September 14, 1816.

Received from Captain Maitland a box, containing four packages, marked each 20,000 francs, and said to contain four thousand Napoleons d'or.

H. Lowe,
Major General.

About eleven a.m., Lord Keith came on board in the *Tonnant*'s barge, to accompany Bonaparte from the *Bellerophon* to the *Northumberland*. Count Bertrand immediately went into the cabin to inform him of his Lordship's arrival: it was, however, full two hours before it was reported that he was ready to attend him. About one o'clock, the barge of the Admiral was prepared;

a Captain's guard turned out, and by Lord Keith's direction, as Napoleon crossed the quarter-deck to leave the ship, the guard presented arms, and three ruffles of the drum were beat, being the salute given to a General Officer.

He walked out of the cabin with a steady, firm step, came up to me, and, taking off his hat, said, "Captain Maitland, I take this last opportunity of once more returning you my thanks for the manner in which you have treated me while on board the *Bellerophon*, and also to request you will convey them to the officers and ship's company you command:" then turning to the Officers, who were standing by me, he added, "Gentlemen, I have requested your Captain to express my gratitude to you for your attention to me, and to those who have followed my fortunes." He then went forward to the gangway; and before he went down the ship's side, bowed two or three times to the ship's company, who were collected in the waist and on the forecastle; he was followed by the ladies and the French Officers, and lastly by Lord Keith. After the boat had shoved off, and got the distance of about thirty yards from the ship, he stood up, pulled his hat off, and bowed first to the Officers, and then to the men; and immediately sat down, and entered into conversation with Lord Keith, with as much apparent composure as if he had been only going from one ship to the other to pay a visit.

About a quarter of an hour before Bonaparte quitted the *Bellerophon*, Montholon came to me on the quarter-deck, and said, "I am directed by the Emperor to return you his thanks for the manner in which you have conducted yourself throughout the whole of this affair; and he desires me to say, that the greatest cause of disappointment he feels in not being admitted to an interview with the Prince Regent is, that he had intended to ask as a favour from his Royal Highness, that you should be promoted to the rank of Rear Admiral." I answered, "that although the request could not have been complied with under any circumstances, as it was contrary to the regulations of our naval service, yet I do not the less feel the kindness of the intention." "He meant also," he said, " to have presented you with a box containing his portrait, but he understands you are determined not to accept it." I replied, "In the situation I am placed, it is quite impossible I can receive any present from him." "He is perfectly aware," said he, "of the delicacy of your situation, and approves of your conduct." I then said, " I feel much hurt that Count Las Cases should have stated to Lord Keith, that I had promised Bonaparte should be well received in England, or indeed made promises of any sort. I have endeavoured to conduct myself with integrity and honour throughout the whole of this transaction, and therefore cannot allow such an assertion to go un-contradicted." "Oh!" said he, "Las Cases negotiated this business; it has turned out very differently from what he and all of us expected. He attributes the Emperor's situation to himself, and is therefore desirous of giving it the

A tumbler given to Captain Maitland by Napoleon bearing the monogram 'J' for Joséphine.

best countenance he can; but I assure you, the Emperor is convinced your conduct has been most honourable": then taking my hand, he pressed it, and added, "and that is my opinion also."

In the course of the afternoon, I attended General Savary and Lallemand on board the *Northumberland*, where they went for the purpose of taking a last farewell of their master. I had very little conversation with him myself, but they remained with him a considerable time. When I was about to return to my ship, I went into the cabin to tell them they must accompany me. They approached him in the after-cabin, where he was standing, when he embraced each of them most affectionately, after the French manner, putting his arms round them, and touching their cheeks with his. He was firm and collected; but, in turning from him, the tears were streaming from their eyes. On getting on board, all the squadron got under weigh, the *Tonnant* and *Bellerophon* to return to Plymouth, the *Northumberland*, with two troop ships in company, to proceed to St Helena. The following day she was joined by a frigate and several sloops of war from Plymouth, when she made sail to the westward.

Having now brought my narrative down to the period of Bonaparte's quitting the ship, it only remains for me to give some account of his person and character, as far as it fell under my view. In doing so, I shall endeavour, as far as possible, in the same spirit with which the foregoing narrative is written, to avoid being biased, either by favourable or unfavourable feelings towards him. What he may have been when at the head of the French Empire, with the destiny of the greater part of Europe under his control, I have no peculiar means of knowing; all I can pretend to do is, to describe him as he was on board the *Bellerophon*; adding a few anecdotes, which have been omitted in the course of the narrative, as serving to throw some further light upon his character.

Napoleon Bonaparte, when he came on board the *Bellerophon*, on the 15th of July, 1815, wanted exactly one month of completing his forty-sixth year, being born the 15th of August, 1769. He was then a remarkably strong, well-built man, about five feet seven inches high, his limbs particularly well-formed, with a fine ankle and very small foot, of which he seemed rather vain, as he always wore, while on board the ship, silk stockings and shoes. His hands were also very small, and had the plumpness of a woman's rather than the robustness of a man's. His eyes light grey, teeth good; and when he smiled, the expression of his countenance was highly pleasing; when under the influence of disappointment, however, it assumed a dark gloomy cast. His hair was of a very dark brown, nearly approaching to black, and, though a little thin on the top and front, had not a grey hair amongst it. His complexion was a very uncommon one, being of a light sallow colour, differing from almost any other I ever met with. From his having become corpulent, he had lost much of his personal activity, and, if we are to give credit to those who attended him, a very considerable portion of his mental energy was also gone. It is certain his habits were very lethargic while he was on board the *Bellerophon*; for though he went to bed between eight and nine o'clock in the evening, and did not rise till about the same hour in the morning, he frequently fell asleep on the sofa in the cabin in the course of the day. His general appearance was that of a man rather older than he then was. His manners were extremely pleasing and affable: he joined in every conversation, related numerous anecdotes, and endeavoured, in every way, to promote good humour: he even admitted his attendants to great familiarity; and I saw one or two instances of their contradicting him in the most direct terms, though they generally treated him with much respect. He possessed, to a wonderful degree, a facility in making a favourable impression upon those with whom he entered into conversation: this appeared to me to be accomplished by turning the subject to matters he supposed the person he was addressing was well acquainted with, and on which he could show himself to advantage. This had the effect of putting him in good humour with himself; after which it was not a very difficult matter to transfer a part of that feeling to the person who had occasioned it. Lord Keith appears to have formed a very high opinion of the fascination of his conversation, and expressed it very emphatically to me, after he had seen him: speaking of his wish for an interview with the Prince Regent, "D—n the fellow," he said, "if he had obtained an interview with his Royal Highness, in half an hour they would have been the best friends in England." He appeared to have great command of temper; for, though no man could have had greater trials than fell to his lot during the time he remained on board the *Bellerophon*, he never, in my presence, or as far as I know, allowed a fretful or captious expression to escape him: even the day he received the notification from Sir Henry Bunbury, that it was determined to send him to St Helena, he chatted and conversed with the same cheerfulness as usual. It has been asserted that he was acting a part all the time he was on board the ship; but still, even allowing that to be the case, nothing but great command of temper could have enabled him to have sustained such a part for so many days, in his situation.

I shall here relate a circumstance that occurred during the passage to England, which will show in a strong point of view the freedom that subsisted between him and those of his attendants in whom he had confidence. A conversation took place respecting the relative state of cultivation in France and in England. My opinion being asked, I said, that though the climate of France was much superior to that of England, I believed that agriculture had arrived at a greater state of perfection with us than in France. Most of the Frenchmen treated the idea with ridicule; upon which I said, let us refer to Monsieur Las Cases, who has lived several years in England. "You are right," said he; "there can be no doubt, that agriculture has arrived to much greater perfection in England than in France; but what I admire most in England, are the country-seats of your noblemen and gentlemen; there you surpass France very much." General Bertrand then took up the conversation, and said, that he was assured, that thirty thousand pounds sterling was annually expended on the park and grounds of Blenheim. Bonaparte immediately reduced that sum into livres; and observed, "The thing is impossible: the English people are not fools; they know the value of money, and no individual either could or would expend such a sum for such a purpose." He then spoke of the expense of keeping up Malmaison, one of the country palaces in France; stating the sum it cost annually, which did not exceed five thousand pounds. Bertrand still persisted in his statement, and made a reference to me. I, however, could give no information further than saying, that from what I had heard of the Duke of Marlborough's finances, he could not possibly lay out any such sum on Blenheim. Monsieur Bertrand would not give up the point, but repeated his assertion. On which Bonaparte said, with quickness, " Bah! c'est impossible." "Oh!" said Bertrand, much offended, "if you are to reply in that manner, there is an end of all argument;" and for some time would not converse with him. Bonaparte, so far from taking umbrage, did all he could to soothe him and restore him to good-humour, which was not very difficult to effect.

One morning he began to talk of his wife and child, and desired Marchand to bring two or three miniature pictures to show me: he spoke of them with much feeling and affection. "I feel," said he, "the conduct of the allied sovereigns to be more cruel and unjustifiable towards me in that respect than in any other. Why should they deprive me of the comforts of domestic society, and take from me what must be the dearest objects of affection to every man—my child, and the mother of that child?" On his expressing himself as above, I looked him steadily in the face, to observe whether he showed any emotion: the tears were standing in his eyes, and the whole of his countenance appeared evidently under the influence of a strong feeling of grief.

There were two pictures of young Napoleon: one in the dress of a Polish lancer, and the other with long curly flowing ringlets: they both represented a fair, strong, chubby boy, with features very much resembling those of his father. That of his mother, a very fair woman, with good features, but by no means handsome.

From the observations I was enabled to make, I very much doubt Monsieur Savary's statement, that the passion of ambition was so completely overcome in his bosom, "that had it been proposed to him again to ascend the throne of France, he would have declined it"; and I do think, that if he had succeeded in eluding the British cruisers and arrived in America, he would always have looked forward to returning to France. In all his conversations, he spoke of ambition as a quality absolutely necessary to form the character of a soldier. On one occasion, Savary spoke of Kléber, (who was left by Napoleon in command of the army when he quitted Egypt,) in terms of high encomium; this brought on a discussion upon the respective merits of that officer and Dessaix, whose aide-de-camp Savary had been during the negotiation of the convention of El Arish. Bonaparte, speaking of Kléber, bestowed upon him great praise as an officer; but he added, "He was deficient in one of the most necessary qualifications of a soldier,—ambition. He was indolent, and required constant spurring. Dessaix, on the contrary, had all his abilities, which were kept in constant activity by a mind whose ambition there was no satisfying; and, had they both lived to the present period, he would have been much the greater man of the two."

It does not appear from the statement of Bonaparte's attendants, that he had made any very considerable provision for the future, in the event of a reverse of fortune. They often regretted his poverty; and Madame Bertrand assured me that he was not possessed of more than a million of francs—forty-two thousand pounds of our money; which, if correct, is certainly not a very large sum for a man who had had so many millions at his disposal.[1] "The Emperor has always declared," she said, "that he would rise or fall with the country, and never would enrich himself out of the public property." He also upon one occasion, when there was some intention of leaving Madame Bertrand with her children in England, after stating Bertrand's poverty as an objection to that arrangement, said to me, "My finances are not such as to enable me to give him much assistance."

Bonaparte's carriage, which was taken at the battle of Waterloo by the

Prussian cavalry, contained many articles of great value. In it was a *necessaire*, in which all the instruments, basin, &c. were composed of gold; a sword set with diamonds, and a diamond necklace, estimated at a very large sum of money, which one of his sisters (I think, the Princess of Borghese) put round his neck the night he took leave of her at Paris, on his setting out to join the army previous to the battle of Waterloo, and which he had taken off and deposited in a secret place in the carriage; Marchand, his valet de chambre, being so nearly taken by the Prussian hussars, that he quitted the carriage without having time to secure it. But I have since learned from Las Cases's *Memoirs*, that the necklace alluded to was saved, and that Las Cases had it concealed about his person all the time he was on board the *Bellerophon*.

It has been stated in many of the public prints, that had not the Marquis of Anglesea received a wound when he was leading on a charge, Bonaparte must have fallen into his hands. In consequence of observing this assertion, I asked Generals Bertrand and Gourgaud whether they knew if any such occurrence had taken place: both of whom replied, "Certainly not; the Emperor was frequently in the midst of the British troops (pêle-mêle avec les troupes Angloises); but at no time during the battle was he in danger of being captured by a charge of cavalry."

The midshipmen of the *Bellerophon* were in the habit of occasionally performing plays, to amuse themselves and the officers during the tedious operations of a blockade. Bonaparte being told of it by Savary, requested that they would oblige him by acting one for his amusement. During the performance, Madame Bertrand sat next to him, and interpreted. He appeared much amused, and laughed very heartily at our ladies, who were personated by great strapping fellows dressed in women's clothes, and not in the most tidy fashion. He had the patience to remain to the end of the third act, though, when attending the Opera at Paris, he had always retired at the end of the first.

I heard several of the French officers discussing the merits of the British troops. One of them said, "The cavalry is superb." I observed, "In England we have a higher opinion of our infantry." "You are right," said he; "there is none such in the world: there is no making an impression on them: you may as well attempt to charge through a wall: and their fire is tremendous." Another of them observed: "A great fault in your cavalry is their not having their horses sufficiently under command: there must be something wrong in the bit; as on one or two occasions in a charge, they could not stop their horses: our troops opened to the right and left, let them pass through, and then closed their ranks again, when they were either killed or taken prisoners."

I never heard Bonaparte speak of the battle of Waterloo, or give an opinion of the Duke of Wellington; but I asked General Bertrand what Napoleon thought of him. "Why," replied he, "I will give you his opinion nearly in the words he delivered it to me. 'The Duke of Wellington, in the management of an army, is fully equal to myself, with the advantage of possessing more prudence.'"

During the time that Bonaparte was on board the *Bellerophon*, we always lived expressly for his accommodation—entirely in the French manner; that is to say, a hot meal was served at ten o'clock in the morning, and another at six in the evening; and so nearly did they resemble each other in all respects, that a stranger might have found difficulty, in coming into the cabin, to distinguish breakfast from dinner. His maître d'hôtel took the joints off the table, cut them up in portions, and then handed them round. Bonaparte ate a great deal, and generally of strong solid food: in drinking he was extremely abstemious, confining himself almost entirely to claret, and seldom taking more than half-a-pint at a meal.

Immediately after dinner, strong coffee was handed round, and then some cordial; after which he rose from table, the whole meal seldom lasting more than twenty or twenty-five minutes: and I was told, that during the time he was at the head of the French Government, he never allowed more than fifteen minutes for that purpose.

After he had quitted the ship, being desirous to know the feeling of the ship's company towards him, I asked my servant what the people said of him. "Why, Sir," he answered, "I heard several of them conversing together about him this morning; when one of them observed, 'Well, they may abuse that man as much as they please; but if the people of England knew him as well as we do, they would not hurt a hair of his head;' in which the others agreed." This was the more extraordinary, as he never went through the ship's company but once, immediately after his coming on board, when I attended him, and he did not speak to any of the men; merely returning their salute by pulling off his hat; and in consequence of his presence, they suffered many privations, such as not being allowed to see their wives and friends, or to go on shore, having to keep watch in port, &c.; and when he left the ship, the only money he distributed was twenty Napoleons to my steward, fifteen to one of the under-servants, and ten to the cook.

It may, perhaps, be interesting to give a slight sketch of the principal persons who accompanied Bonaparte to the *Bellerophon*; premising, that I do not pretend to be minutely correct in the view I took of them: the trying circumstances in which these unfortunate men were placed, being such as required more than common temper; and I think it very doubtful, whether, in the same situation, Englishmen would have maintained equal forbearance.

Count Bertrand was a man of about forty-four years of age, five feet ten inches in height, of a slight make and prepossessing appearance: his manners extremely placid and gentle, though evidently of a warm temper; and showed himself rather hasty in his conduct to Sir George Cockburn, about searching the baggage; as Sir George was not acting upon his own authority, but by the directions of his superiors, and was inclined to conduct himself with as much consideration as his orders would admit. He was an affectionate attentive husband, and much attached to his children.

The Countess Bertrand was then of a tall, slight figure. Her maiden name was Dillon; her father was an Irishman in the French service, who lost his life during the revolution, and was related to Lord Dillon. Though, perhaps, a little warm, she has undoubtedly many excellent qualities: she showed herself to be a kind mother and affectionate wife; and if she easily took offence, she as easily forgot it; and any little dispute that occurred between her and me, was amply atoned for by the frank and affectionate manner in which she took leave when we were about to part, perhaps for ever. They had, at the time I speak of, three fine children,—two boys and a girl; the eldest boy about five years of age, who seemed to have a natural turn for the profession of his father: his constant amusement, in which the young lady and little Montholon joined, was forming lines and squares, and other military evolutions, on the quarter-deck.

General Savary, Duc de Rovigo, was a tall handsome man, then about forty-six years of age, of a cheerful disposition; and notwithstanding the alarm he was in lest he should be given up to the French Government, he never forgot himself so far as to make use of a rude expression in my presence. He was Minister of Police after Fouché. As a great deal had been said about Captain Wright's death, I spoke to him one day upon the subject, and told him it was generally believed in England that he had been murdered: he said, "I took much pains in investigating that matter, and in ascertaining the cause of his death; and I have not a doubt that he cut his own throat in a fit of delirium." Neither Savary nor Lallemand were allowed to accompany Bonaparte to St Helena; but on the *Bellerophon*'s return to Plymouth, after transferring Napoleon to the *Northumberland*, both of them, together with Planat and the other officers with the exception of three, were, by an order from the Admiralty, sent on board the *Eurotas* frigate, which conveyed them to Malta, from whence, after remaining some time as prisoners in Fort St Angelo, they were allowed to proceed to Smyrna.[2]

General Lallemand[3] was about forty-two years of age, of a thick strong make; his manners not pleasing, and his appearance by no means prepossessing. During the whole time he was in the *Bellerophon*, he was morose and abstracted, and seemed much alarmed lest he should be given up to the French Government; and there can be little doubt, had he fallen into its power, he would have shared the fate of Ney, as he had, with the troops under his command, joined Napoleon on his return from Elba. He had formerly been, for several years, one of Bonaparte's aide-de-camps, and during the time he was in the *Bellerophon* always did that duty in rotation with Montholon and Gourgaud; one of them sleeping in his clothes on a mattress every night outside of the door of the cabin he slept in. The other two aide-de-camps, Generals Montholon[4] and Gourgaud,[5] were young men about thirty-two years of age, the former an officer in the cavalry, and the other in the artillery: they were both of good families; but their attachment to Bonaparte induced them to give up their country and property to follow him.

Madame Montholon was a quiet unassuming woman, gave no trouble, and seemed perfectly satisfied, provided she were allowed to accompany her husband. She had with her one fine little boy, about four years old, and I believe left another child at nurse in France.

Count Las Cases, though he bore the title of Counsellor of State, held no official situation with Bonaparte; nor did I perfectly understand how he came to accompany him on his departure from France, as he was not with him in Elba: but the intimacy appeared to have been formed since his return from that island. Napoleon was fond of his conversation. He was of small stature, being little more than five feet high, and slightly made. He always spoke of his master in terms of enthusiasm, and resisted every application from his wife and family to remain behind, being determined to follow wherever Bonaparte might be sent. He took with him his eldest son, a quick intelligent boy of thirteen.

Monsieur Maingaut, the surgeon, with all the domestics beyond the twelve who went to St Helena, were conveyed in the *Bellerophon* to Portsmouth, and from thence sent to Cherbourg, and landed there. Monsieur Saint Catharine, a lad about sixteen, nephew to the Empress Josephine, and a native of Martinique, was provided with a passage to that island in one of our sloops of war.

Captain Piontowski,[6] a Pole, was allowed to proceed to St Helena, some time after the *Northumberland* sailed. Why this indulgence was granted to him, I never clearly understood; but it was said to be in consequence of the representations he made to the British Government, of the very strong attachment he entertained to his fallen master,—a feeling, as far as I could judge, which prevailed with equal force in the breasts of all those who accompanied him from France, without excepting Madame Bertrand, who, when not influenced by the horror she entertained of being banished to St Helena, always spoke of him not only with affection, but in the language of respect and enthusiasm.

Appendix I

So many erroneous statements have gone abroad, as to the terms of Bonaparte's reception on board the *Bellerophon*, that I conceive it right to give the following correspondence, although at the expense of some repetition; in order to its being distinctly seen, that the good faith of the British nation was not compromised on that occasion, but that His Majesty's Government were at perfect liberty, as far as those terms were concerned, to act as they thought best.

Tonnent, at anchor under Berry-head,
7th August, 1815,

SIR,

Count Las Cases having this morning stated to me that he understood from you, when he was on board the *Bellerophon* in Basque Roads, on a mission from General Bonaparte, that you were authorized to receive the General and his suite on board the ship you command, for conveyance to England; and that you assured him, at the same time, that both the General and his suite would be well received there; you are to report for my information, such observations as you may consider it necessary to make upon these assertions,

I am, Sir,
Your most obedient, humble servant,
KEITH, Admiral.

Captain Maitland, Bellerophon.

H.M.S. Bellerophon,
Plymouth Sound, 8th August, 1815.

My LORD,

I have to acknowledge the receipt of your Lordship's letter of yesterday's date, informing me that Count Las Cases had stated to you, that he had understood from me when he was on board the Bellerophon in Basque Roads, on a mission from General Bonaparte, that I was authorized to receive the General and his suite on board the ship I command, for a conveyance to England, and that I assured him at the same time, that both the General and his suite would be well received there; and directing me to report for your Lordship's information such observations as I may consider it necessary to make upon these assertions. I shall, in consequence, state, to the best of my recollection, the whole of the transaction that took place between Count Las Cases and me, on the 14th of July, respecting the embarkation of Napoleon Bonaparte, for the veracity of which I beg to refer your Lordship to Captain Sartorius as to what was said in the morning, and to that officer and Captain Gambier (the Myrmidon having joined me in the afternoon) as to what passed in the evening.

Your Lordship being informed already of the flag of truce that came out to me on the 10th of July, as well as of every thing that occurred on that occasion, I shall confine myself to the transactions of the 14th of the same month.

Early in the morning of that day, the officer of the watch informed me, a schooner, bearing a flag of truce, was approaching: on her joining the ship, about seven a.m. the Count Las Cases and General Lallemand came on board, when, on being shown into the cabin, Las Cases asked me if any answer had been returned to the letter sent by me to Sir Henry Hotham respecting Napoleon Bonaparte being allowed to pass for America, either in the frigates or in a neutral vessel. I informed him no answer had been returned, though I hourly expected, in consequence of those despatches, Sir Henry Hotham would arrive; and, as I had told Monsieur Las Cases, when last on board, that I should send my boat in when the answer came, it was quite unnecessary to have sent out a flag of truce on that account:—there, for the time, the conversation terminated. On their coming on board, I had made the signal for the Captain of the Slaney, being desirous of having a witness to all that might pass.

After breakfast (during which Captain Sartorius came on board) we retired to the after-cabin, when Monsieur Las Cases began on the same subject, and said, 'The Emperor was so anxious to stop the further effusion of blood, that he would go to America in any way the English Government would sanction, either in a neutral, a disarmed frigate, or an English ship of war.' To which I replied, 'I have no authority to permit any of those measures; but if he chooses to come on board the ship I command, I think, under the orders I am acting with, I may venture to receive him and carry him to England; but, if I do so, I can in no way be answerable for the reception he may meet with (this I repeated several times); when Las Cases said, 'I have little doubt, under those circumstances, that you will see the Emperor on board the Bellerophon: After some more general conversation, and the above being frequently repeated, Monsieur Las Cases and General Lallemand took their leave: and I assure your Lordship that I never, in any way, entered into conditions with respect to the reception General Bonaparte was to meet with; nor was it, at that time, finally arranged that he was to come on board the Bellerophon. In the course of conversation, Las Cases asked me whether I thought Bonaparte would be well received in England; to which I gave the only answer I could do in my situation—'That I did not at all know what was the intention of the British Government; but I had no reason to suppose he would not be well received: It is here worthy of remark, that when Las Cases came on board, he assured me that Bonaparte was then at Rochefort, and that it would be necessary for him to go there to report the conversation that had passed between us (this I can prove by the testimony of Captain Sartorius, and the first Lieutenant of this ship, to whom I spoke of it at the time), which statement was not fact; Buonaparte never having quitted Isle d'Aix, or the frigates, after the 3rd.

I was, therefore, much surprised at seeing Monsieur Las Cases on board again before seven o'clock the same evening; and one of the first questions I put to him was, whether he had been at Rochefort. He answered, that on returning to Isle d'Aix, he found that Bonaparte had arrived there.

Monsieur Las Cases then presented to me the letter Count Bertrand wrote concerning Bonaparte's intention to come on board the ship (a copy of which has been transmitted to your Lordship by Sir Henry Hotham); and it was not till then agreed upon that I should receive him; when either Monsieur Las Cases, or General Gourgaud (I am not positive which, as I was employed writing my own despatches), wrote to Bertrand to inform him of it. While paper was preparing to write the letter, I said again to Monsieur Las Cases, 'You will recollect I have no authority for making conditions of any sort.' Nor has Monsieur Las Cases ever started such an idea till the day before yesterday. That it was not the feeling of Bonaparte, or the rest of his people, I will give strong proof, drawn from the conversations they have held with me.

As I never heard the subject mentioned till two days ago, I shall not detail every conversation that has passed, but confine myself to that period.

The night that the squadron anchored at the back of Berry-head, Bonaparte sent for me about 10 p.m. and said he was informed by Bertrand, that I had received orders to remove him to the *Northumberland,* and wished to know if that was the case; on being told that it was, he requested I would write a letter to Bertrand, stating I had such orders, that it might not appear that he went of his own accord, but that he had been forced to do so. I told him, I could have no objection, and wrote a letter to that effect (a copy of which is here annexed), which your Lordship afterwards sanctioned, and desired me, if he required it, to give him a copy of the order.

After having arranged that matter, I was going to withdraw, when he requested me to remain, as he had something more to say: he then began complaining of his treatment in being forced to go to St Helena: among other things, he observed, 'They say I made no conditions: certainly, I made no conditions: how could a private man (*un particulier*) make conditions with a nation? I wanted nothing from them but hospitality, or (as the ancients would express it) air and water. I threw myself on the generosity of the English nation; I claimed a place *sur leurs foyers*, and my only wish was to purchase a small estate and end my life in tranquillity.' After more of the same sort of conversation I left him for the night.

On the morning he removed from the *Bellerophon* to the *Northumberland,* he sent for me again, and said, 'I have sent for you to express my gratitude for your conduct to me, while I have been on board the ship you command. My reception in England has been very different from what I expected; but you throughout have behaved like a man of honour; and I request you will accept my thanks, as well as convey them to the officers, and ship's company of the *Bellerophon.*'

Soon afterwards Montholon came to me from Bonaparte; but, to understand what passed between him and me, I must revert to a conversation that I had with Madame Bertrand on the passage from Rochefort.

It is not necessary to state how the conversation commenced, as it does not apply to the present transaction; but she informed me, that it was Bonaparte's intention to present me with a box containing his picture set with diamonds. I answered, 'I hope not, for I cannot receive it.'

'Then you will offend him very much,' she said. 'If that is the case,' I replied, 'I request you will take measures to prevent its being offered, as it is absolutely impossible I can accept of it; and I wish to spare him the mortification, and myself the pain, of a refusal.' There the matter dropt, and I heard no more of it, till about half an hour before Bonaparte quitted the *Bellerophon,* when Montholon came to me, and said he was desired by Bonaparte to express the high sense he entertained of my conduct throughout the whole of the transaction: that it had been his intention to present me with a box containing his portrait, but that he understood I was determined not to accept it. I said, 'Placed as I was, I felt it impossible to receive a present from him, though I was highly flattered at the testimony he had borne to the uprightness of my conduct throughout' Montholon then added, 'One of the greatest causes of chagrin he feels in not being admitted to an interview with the Prince Regent, is, that he had determined to ask as a favour, your being promoted to the rank of Rear Admiral.' To which I replied, 'That would have been quite impossible, but I do not the less feel the kindness of the intention.' I then said, 'I am hurt that Las Cases should say I held forth any assurances as to the reception Buonaparte was to meet with in England.' 'Oh!' said he, 'Las Cases is disappointed in his expectations; and as he negotiated the affair, he attributes the Emperor's situation to himself: but I can assure you, that he (Bonaparte) feels convinced you have acted like a man of honour throughout'

As your Lordship overheard part of a conversation which took place between Las Cases and me on the quarter-deck of the *Bellerophon*, I shall not detail it; but on that occasion, I positively denied having promised anything as to the reception of Bonaparte and his suite; and I believe your Lordship was of opinion he could not make out the statement to you.

It is extremely unpleasant for me to be under the necessity of entering into a detail of this sort; but the unhandsome representation Monsieur Las Cases has made to your Lordship of my conduct, has obliged me to produce proofs of the light in which the transaction was viewed by Bonaparte as well as his attendants.

I again repeat, that Captains Gambier and Sartorius can verify the principal part of what I have stated, as far as concerns the charge made against me by Count Las Cases.

> I have the honour to be,
> > Your Lordship's Most obedient humble servant,
> > > FREDERICK L. MAITLAND.

To the Right Hon. Viscount Keith, G.C.B.
&c. &c. &c.

> > > Slaney, in Plymouth Sound, 15th August, 1815.

MY LORD,

I have read Captain Maitland's letter to your Lordship, of the 8th instant, containing his observations upon the assertions made on the preceding day by Count Las Cases; and I most fully attest the correctness of the statement he has made, so far as relates to the conversations that took place in my presence.

I have the honour to be, Your Lordship's Most obedient humble servant,

G. R. SARTORIUS,
Capt. of H.M.S. Slaney.

To the Right Hon. Viscount Keith, G.C.B. &c. &c. &c.

A letter to the same effect as the foregoing was written to Lord Keith, by Captain Gambier, of the *Myrmidon*, and forwarded by his Lordship to the Admiralty, with my report; of which, by some accident, the Admiral's secretary did not furnish me with a copy.

Appendix II

List of Officers borne on the Books of HMS *Bellerophon* in July 1815.

Captain Fred. L. Maitland.
Lieutenant Andrew Mott.[7]
Lieutenant William Walford.
Lieutenant John Bowerbank.
Lieutenant Gabriel Christie.
Lieutenant Edward William Ramsay.
Captain of Marines, George Marshall.
Lieutenant of Marines, J. W. Simpson.
Lieutenant Henry Smith.
Master, Stephen Vale.
Surgeon, Barry O'Meara.
Assistant-Surgeon, A. Milne.
Assistant-Surgeon, E. Graebke.
Chaplain, J. W. Wynne.
Purser, George Jackson.

Appendix III

Letter from Ephraim Graebke, assistant-surgeon on board HMS *Bellerophon*, to his mother, giving an account of Napoleon's surrender (British Museum, Additional MSS. 34,710, f. 81).

H.M.S. Bellerophon, Plymouth Sound, Tuesday, July 30, 1815.

My Dear Mother,

You will be surprised at not hearing from me, and knowing the Bellerophon's arrival in England, but when I tell you no private letters were allowed to leave the ship before today, that will cease. It's unnecessary to say that we have got Bonaparte and suite on board, as it was known in England previous to our arrival, which took place on the 24th instant in Torbay. The circumstances which led to his surrender were his defeats in all points, and was it not for the strict blockade we kept up would [*sic*] have escaped to America. We heard of his being on board the French frigate Saale off Rochfort, from which moment we watched his movements if possible more closely than before. On the morning of the 14th instant, observing a schooner bearing a flag of truce on board standing towards us, we hove to for her, when Count Lascazas and General Lallemande came on board with proposals from Buonaparte, in consequence of which we came to anchor in the evening in the roads off Rochelle. Next morning, 15th instant, at 4 a.m. observed a man-of-war brig standing out and beating towards us, we immediately dispatched all our boats. Lieut. Mott in the barge brought Buonaparte on board at 7, the boats were busily employed in bringing his retinue and baggage, and I never saw men exert themselves so much as ours did that day, lest Admiral Hotham should take him, as he was off the harbour in the Superb, and saw him coming on board here, and did all in his power to get in, but did not come to anchor before 11 in the forenoon. Buonaparte is a fine-looking man, inclined to corpulency, is five feet six inches in height, his hair turning grey,[8] and a little bald on the crown of the head, no whiskers, complexion French yellow, eyes grey, Roman nose, good mouth and chin, neck short, big belly, arms stout, small white hands, and shews a good leg. He wears a cocked hat somewhat like our old-fashioned three cornered ones, with the tricoloured cockade in it, plain green coat, cape red, and cuffs the same, plain gold epaulets, and a large star on the left breast, white waistcoat and breeches and white silk stockings, thin shoes and buckles. Eats but two meals in the day, breakfast and dinner, and these are sumptuous, fish, flesh, and fowl, wines, fruit, various French dishes &c. &c. He breakfasts about eleven and dines at six, is about half an hour at each, when he generally comes on deck or goes into the after-cabin to study. We do not know what's to be done with him yet, he remains on board until we hear from the allies. In his suite are Marshal Bertrand, Duc de Rovigo [Savary] once the French minister of police, Counts Lascazas and Montholon, Generals Lallemande and Gourgou, several Lieut.-Colonels and Captains, to enumerate them would be tedious. We have 33 on board, 17 were sent on board the Myrmidon, Captn. Gambier. There are two Countesses on board, but not to be compared even to our English ladies. Their children are handsome. . . . We performed the comedy of the "Poor Gentleman" before Bonaparte and suite. I acted the part of Corporal Foss. It went off very well, our scenery was excellent. The female dresses were badly suited for Midshipmen. I long to hear from you and will expect to hear all the news. . . . I wish you were all here to see Buonaparte, the curiosity of all ranks to see him is excessive. There are Admiralty orders not to allow any person whatever on board, but they crowd in boats round the ship, and he very condescendingly stands looking at them through a spyglass. There are two frigates, one on each side of us, the Eurotas and Liffey, and their boats are constantly rowing about the ship to keep off the boats. We prisoners have no other amusement than to look at them contending for places. I hope we will soon be allowed to go ashore, as I want to see Captain Sandys. You must be tired reading this long epistle. We took some prizes, one ship laden with Buonaparte's soldiers, one chasse maree laden with resin, and the Cephulus man-of-war brig sent in a West Indiaman laden with sugar, coffee, &c. from Martinique bound to France, and for which we will share by mutual agreements. Give my affectionate love to Ally, Anne, Wilhelmina, Sophia and Jane. I know the want of not being near them as my shirts are going to pieces, as soon as I can afford the sum I will get some new ones. I have the old number the same as when

I left you and bought none since. . . . I remain, my dear mother, your affectionate son,

Ephraim Graebke

P.S.—I think myself very lucky to belong to the old Bellerophon at this important time. Lose no time in answering this letter.

Mrs Graebke,
Midleton, Co. Cork.

Appendix IV

Extracts from *Memoirs of an Aristocrat, and Reminiscences of the Emperor Napoleon, by a Midshipman of the Bellerophon*, George Home, 1838.

About six in the morning, the look-out man at the mast-head announced a large ship of war standing direct in for the roadstead, which Captain Maitland, suspecting to be the Superb, bearing the flag of Admiral Sir Henry Hotham, he gave immediate orders to hoist out the barge, and dispatched her, under the command of the first lieutenant, to the French brig, being apprehensive that if the Admiral arrived before the brig got out, that Napoleon would deliver himself up to the Admiral instead of us, and thus have lost us so much honour.

As our barge approached, the brig hove to, and from the moment she came alongside, we watched every motion with deep anxiety. Like all Napoleon's movements, he was not slow even in this, his last free act. The barge had not remained ten minutes alongside, before we saw the rigging of the brig crowded with men, persons stepping down the side into the boat, and the next moment she shoved off; and gave way for the ship; while the waving of the men's hats in the rigging, and the cheering which we heard faintly in the distance, left no doubt that the expected guest was approaching. A general's guard of marines was ordered aft on the quarter-deck, and the boatswain stood, whistle in hand, ready to do the honours of the side. The lieutenants stood grouped first on the quarter-deck, and we more humble middies behind them, while the captain, evidently in much anxiety, kept trudging backwards and forwards between the gangway and his own cabin, sometimes peeping out at one of the quarter-deck ports, to see if the barge was drawing near.

It is a sin to mix up any trifling story with so great an event; but a circumstance occurred so laughable of itself, rendered more so from the solemnity of the occasion, that I cannot resist mentioning it. While in this state of eager expectation, a young midshipman, one of the Bruces of Kennet, I think, walked very demurely up to Manning, the boatswain, who was standing all importance at the gangway, and after comically eyeing his squat figure and bronzed countenance, Bruce gently laid hold of one of his whiskers, to which the boatswain good-naturedly submitted, as the youngster was a great favourite with him.

'Manning,' says he, most sentimentally, 'this is the proudest day of your life; you are this day to do the honours of the side to the greatest man the world ever produced or ever will produce.'

Here the boatswain eyed him with proud delight. 'And along with the great Napoleon, the name of Manning, the boatswain of the Bellerophon, will go down to the latest posterity; and, as a relic of that great man, permit me, my dear Manning, to preserve a lock of your hair.'

Here he made an infernal tug at the boatswain's immense whisker, and fairly carried away a part of it, making his way through the crowd, and down below with the speed of an arrow. The infuriated boatswain, finding he had passed so rapidly from the sublime to the ridiculous, through the instrumentality of this imp of a youngster, could vent his rage in no way but by making his glazed hat spin full force after his tantalizer, with a 'G—d d—n your young eyes and limbs.' The hat, however, fell far short of young Bruce, and the noise and half burst of laughter the trick occasioned drew the attention of the Captain, who, coming up, with a 'What, what's all this?' the poor boatswain was glad to draw to his hat and resume his position.

The barge approached, and ranged alongside. The first lieutenant came up the side, and to Maitland's eager and blunt question, 'Have you got him?' he answered in the affirmative. After the lieutenant came Savary, followed by Marshal Bertrand, who bowed and fell back a pace on the gangway to await the ascent of their master. And now came the little great man himself, wrapped up in his gray greatcoat buttoned to the chin, three-cocked hat and Hussar boots, without any sword, I suppose as emblematical of his changed condition. Maitland received him with every mark of respect, as far as look and deportment could indicate; but he was not received with the respect due to a crowned head, which was afterwards insidiously thrown out against Maitland. So far from that, the captain, on Napoleon's addressing him, only moved his hat, as to a general officer, and remained covered while the Emperor spoke to him. His expressions were brief, I believe only reiterating what he had stated the day previous in his letter to the Prince Regent, 'That he placed himself under the protection of the British nation, and under that of the British commander as the representative of his sovereign.' The captain again moved his hat, and turned to conduct the Emperor to the cabin. As he passed through the officers assembled on the quarter-deck, he repeatedly bowed slightly to us, and smiled. What an ineffable beauty there was in that smile, his teeth were finely set, and as white as ivory, and his mouth had a charm about it that I have never seen in any other human countenance. I marked his fine robust figure as he followed Captain Maitland into the cabin, and, boy as I was, I said to myself, 'Now have I a tale for futurity.'

.   .   .   .   .

I shall never forget that morning we made Ushant. I had come on deck at four in the morning to take the morning watch, and the washing of decks had just begun, when, to my astonishment, I saw the Emperor come out of the cabin at that early hour, and make for the poop-ladder. Had I known what human misery is as well as I do now, when I have myself experienced the most cruel injustice and persecution on a lesser scale, the restlessness of Napoleon, or his being unable to close an eye, would have in no way surprised me. If a petty care can break our sleep, what must have been his feeling who had lost the fairest empire on the face of the globe; nay, who had lost a world? From the wetness of the decks, he was in danger of falling at every step, and I immediately stepped up to him, hat in hand, and tendered him my arm, which he laid hold of at once, smiling, and pointing to the poop, saying in broken English, "the poop, the poop"; he ascended the poop-ladder leaning on my arm; and having gained the deck, he quitted his hold and mounted upon a gun-slide, nodding and smiling thanks, for my attention, and pointing to the land he said, 'Ushant, Cape Ushant.' I replied, 'Yes, sire;' and withdrew. He then took out a pocket-glass and applied it to his eye, looking eagerly at the land. In this position, he remained from five in the morning to nearly mid-day, without paying any attention to what was passing around him, or speaking to one of his suite, who had been standing behind him for several hours.

No wonder he thus gazed, it was the last look of the land of his glory, and I am convinced he felt it such. What must have been his feelings in those few hours, how painful the retrospect, and how awful the look forward!—*there* still lay before him that land which he had made so famous, where his proud name had risen until it 'oershadowed the earth with his fame'; there had he been worshipped almost as a god, and bowed to by every servile knee, that now, in the hour of bitter adversity, had basely deserted and betrayed him. Never man was read such a lesson as must have passed before him in that brief space, unless, really, that the greatness of the change, the suddenness of the fall had benumbed all feeling, and left him only a mass of contending passions which combated and stilled each other by the very violence of their working. But this was not the case with Napoleon, his emotion was visible, he hung upon the land until it looked only a speck in the distance, and then, turning, stepped from the gun-slide into the arms of his faithful Bertrand, who stood ready to receive his fallen master. He uttered not a word as he tottered down the poop-ladder, his head hung heavily forward, so as to render his countenance scarcely visible, and in this way he was conducted to his cabin.

.   .   .   .   .

Amongst other plans for killing the, time, and lightening the tedium of a sea passage to the refugees, we bethought us of getting up a play. This was managed by one of the lieutenants of marines, a fellow of great taste, and some one or two of the midshipmen, who pretended to skill in the Shakespearian art. What the piece was I do not recollect,[9] but when it was announced to the Emperor, by Captain Maitland, and the immortal honour of his imperial presence begged, for a few minutes, he laughed very heartily, consented instantly; and turning to Lady Bertrand, told her that she must stand his interpreter. The stage was fitted up between decks, more, I am afraid, in ship-shape than theatrical style; and, sure enough, Napoleon and his whole suite attended. He was much amused with those who took the female parts, which, by the way, was the most smooth-chinned of our young gentlemen, remarking that they were rather a little Dutch built for fine ladies; and, after good-naturedly sitting for nearly twenty minutes, he rose, smiled to the actors, and retired.[10] I mention these circumstances, by way of showing the last glimpses of sunshine that enlivened the exile's closing scene.

On the 23rd, we made the land; and, on the 24th, at seven p.m., we came to an anchor in Torbay, when the first lieutenant was immediately put on shore, with orders to proceed by land to Plymouth, with dispatches for Lord Keith, at that time admiral on the Plymouth station.

I happened to be midshipman of the boat, which conveyed the first lieutenant on shore; and no sooner had we got clear of him, than I was taken prisoner by some twenty young ladies, marched off to a fine house in the little town, regaled with tea and clouted cream, and bored with five thousand questions about Napoleon, the ridiculousness of which I have often laughed at since. 'What like was he—was he really a man? Were his hands and clothes all over blood when he came on board? Was it true that he had killed three horses in riding from Waterloo to the Bellerophon? Were we not all frightened for him? Was his voice like thunder? Could I possibly get them a sight of the monster, just that they might be able to say they had seen him?' etc. etc. I assured those inquisitive nymphs, that the reports they had heard were all nonsense; that the Emperor was not only a man, but a very handsome man too; young withal, had no more blood upon his hands or clothes than was now upon their pure white dresses; that if by chance they got a look of him at the gangway, they would fall in love with him directly; that so far from his hands being red with blood, they were as small, white, and soft as their own charming fingers, and his voice, instead of resembling thunder, was as sweet and musical as their own. This account of the Emperor's beauty perfectly astonished the recluses of Torbay; some misbelieved altogether, while the curiosity of others was excited beyond all bounds. A general proposition was now made, that I should bundle them, like live cattle, into my little cutter, and take them all on board to gratify their curiosity at once. This was quite contrary to orders. Not a soul was allowed to come on board the ship, and I had to plead a thousand excuses for my want of gallantry, in not complying with the very natural wish of my young companions. As far as I was concerned, resistance was vain; I was again seized, hurried down to the boat, and had the pleasure of seeing it filled to cramming with the charmers of Torbay. This was a devil of a mess; I might as well have gone into the mouth of a cannon, as have carried such a cargo alongside the ship,—the thing was impossible. So I had nothing for it, but to call aside the boat's crew, and whisper to them to use gentle violence with my young boarders, and set them down on shore. This was glorious fun to Jack; to work they fell, and in the midst of screams, laughter, and a few d—n my eyes, ma'am, don't kick so hard, on the part of the Bellerophons, we had our nymphs safely deposited on terra firma, and were off in a trice, enjoying the general discomfiture of the poor ladies, who were equally laughed at by the lookers-on, on shore. . . . We left Torbay, on the 26th July at 4 a.m., and at 4 in the evening came to an anchor in Plymouth Sound, just within the breakwater, then only beginning to shew its head above water at low tide. It has since, I am told, been made a splendid affair; but it then only afforded footing for a few gazers from the shore, who perched themselves upon it to watch the cabin-windows of the Bellerophon, in hopes of getting a glimpse of the Emperor.

.   .   .   .   .

The signal for the Emperor's being on deck was the officers uncovering. No sooner was this ceremony noticed, than the rush from without took place, and the screaming and swearing commenced, which was very considerably heightened upon one occasion by a plan of some of our wise-headed young gentlemen. Being in want of amusement, they bethought them of priming the fire engine, which happened to be standing on the poop, and after clapping a relay of hands ready to ply it to advantage, we uncovered, and waited the approach of the boats. No sooner were they within reach, than off went the water-spout, which fell 'alike on the just and the unjust,' for both the dockyard men and the spectators who came within its compass got a good ducking. This prank created an infernal confusion, and our trick having been twigged by the first lieutenant, the chief actors in this notable exploit were ordered up to the mast-head to enjoy their frolic for a few hours, which evidently much gratified the unfortunate sufferers from the effects of the operation.

.   .   .   .   .

Maitland, knowing how he stood with 'the powers that be,' was determined not to commit himself by accepting of any present of value from Napoleon, as he knew it would be directly made a handle of to injure his character as a British officer. He, therefore, I believe, refused to accept of a gold snuff-box tendered him by the Emperor as a mark of his esteem, but he did not refuse the offer of a few dozens of French wine, as a present to Mrs Maitland, who had been personally introduced to Napoleon, as far as introduction was possible, that is, she had been permitted to come within a foot or two of the ship, and Napoleon most condescendingly stepped to the gangway, smiled and bowed to her. Mrs Maitland was a charming little woman in those days,—alas! we are all getting old now,—a daughter of green Erin, and Napoleon seemed greatly pleased with her appearance, hence the offer of this trifling present as a token of respect. The captain took it on shore in the gig, and no sooner had she struck the beach than the custom-house officers jumped on board, and made a seizure of it, hauled the boat up upon the beach, and clapped his Majesty's broad arrow upon her, that fatal mark indicative of being in 'the hands of the Philistines' of the revenue. I shall never forget Maitland's countenance when he came on board after this ridiculous and provoking affair. Being deprived of his own boat by 'the landsharks,' he was obliged to hire a shore boat to bring off himself and his boat's crew, and she was nearly alongside before the first lieutenant discovered that there was a naval officer in her, and on taking a look with his glass, he exclaimed, 'Good God! there is the captain coming off in a shore boat' The side was manned, and when Maitland stepped on board, he turned to Mott with a most rueful countenance, remarking, 'they have seized the wine:' This was petty work, and to make the thing more provoking, they had poor Maitland stuck up next day in the Plymothian journals as having been detected in the act of conveying wine and other presents on shore, received from Napoleon. What was the fate of the wine, I do not know, but the gig, of course, was restored immediately, and I should suppose the wine also, considering the shameful nature of the seizure.

On the 4th of August we left Plymouth Sound in company with the Tonnant, bearing the flag of Admiral Lord Keith, and on the 6th we came to an anchor off Berry-head, there to wait the arrival of the Northumberland, which was hourly expected. She made her appearance in the course of the day, and after due salutes from both admiral's ships, in which noisy greeting we of course joined, for we are very polite at sea, in our own thundering way, she took up her station close by us.

Towards evening Lord Keith came on board of us, and had a long personal interview with Napoleon in the cabin, which we may judge was not of the pleasantest nature. From some intemperate threat of Savary, I believe, who had declared that he would not allow his master to leave the Bellerophon alive, to go into such wretched captivity, it was judged proper to deprive the refugees of their arms. A good many swords, and several brace of pistols, marked with a large silver N. at the butt end, were brought down to the gun-room, where they remained for some hours. Three of the swords belonged to Napoleon, and two of them were pointed out to us as those he wore at Marengo and Austerlitz.

I never in my life felt such a strong inclination to lay my hands on what was not my own. A sword I durst not think of, but could I have got a brace of pistols, or even one solitary pistol, belonging to Napoleon, I would have thought myself the happiest man alive; but it would not do, detection was certain, and with bitter vexation I saw them carried out of the gun-room. Now, reader, do you think this would have been a pardonable theft? Their value was nothing in my eyes; it was a relic of the great man I wanted, and I cared not what it was, or how I came by it; therefore, had I been able to secure a pistol, my conscience would never have smote me with having done wrong; and I am sure, could the Emperor have known with what a pure spirit of devotion I meant to commit the theft, he would have ordered me a brace instantly.

It was this night settled that our surgeon, Barry O'Meara, who afterwards became so conspicuous for his spirited defence of his patient against the tyranny of Sir Hudson Lowe (I hate to write that man's name,) should follow Napoleon to St Helena in the character of surgeon, his own, who looked a poor creature, and was continually sea-sick while on board, having declined, I believe, to accompany him farther, and the 7th was appointed for Napoleon leaving the ship.

The 7th came; it was a dull cloudy sunless day, and every countenance was overcast with gloom. We had not seen the Emperor for a week, and we were all anxious to observe the change that the horrible tidings of his destination had made upon him. Lord Keith, Admiral Cockburn, and Captain Ross,

Vice Admiral Charles Bayne Hodgson Ross CB, (1776-1849). Ross joined the Royal Navy in 1788 and served throughout the Napoleonic Wars. Promoted to captain in 1802, he was given command of HMS *Pique* and captured the French brigs *Phaeton* and *Voltageur* in March 1806. He served in operations in North America in 1814 and later commanded HMS *Northumberland* as captain and transported Napoleon to exile. He later served as Commissioner of Plymouth Dockyard in 1829 and was appointed Commander-in-Chief, Pacific Station in 1837.

came on board about eleven o'clock; and it was intimated to Napoleon, that they were ready to conduct him on board the Northumberland. A general's guard of marines was drawn up on the quarter-deck, to receive him as he came out of the cabin; while part of his suite, and we officers, were ranged about, anxiously waiting the appearance of the future exile of St Helena.

Napoleon was long of attending to the intimation of the Admiral's; and upon Cockburn's becoming impatient, and remarking to old Lord Keith that he should be put in mind, Keith replied, 'No, no, much greater men than either you or I have waited longer for him before now; let him take his time, let him take his time.' This was nobly said of the fine old Scotchman; and although Cockburn and I are blood relations, and I have a particular penchant for my lineage, I cannot help remarking that his manner denoted a great want of feeling. I suppose he was pitched upon by Castlereagh as a proper tool to execute his harsh commands.

At length Napoleon appeared, but oh, how sadly changed from the time we had last seen him on deck. Though quite plain, he was scrupulously cleanly in his person and dress, but that had been forgot, his clothes were ill put on, his beard unshaved, and his countenance pale and haggard. There was a want of firmness in his gait; his brow was overcast, and his whole visage bespoke the deepest melancholy; and it needed but a glance to convince the most careless observer that Napoleon considered himself a doomed man. In this trying hour, however, he lost not his courtesy or presence of mind; instinctively he raised his hat to the guard of marines, when they presented arms as he passed, slightly inclined his head, and even smiled to us officers as he passed through us, returned the salute of the admirals with calm dignity, and, walking up to Captain Maitland, addressed him with great eagerness for nearly ten minutes.

How distinct is every feature, every trait, every line of that majestic countenance in my mind's eye at this moment, now that two-and-twenty years have passed away; but who could witness such a scene and ever forget it? The Romans said that a 'great man struggling with adversity was a sight that the gods looked on with pleasure.' Here, indeed, was adversity, and here was true greatness struggling against it; but to a mere mortal it was a heart-rending sight. The ship's deck looked like a place of execution, and we only wanted the headsman, his block, and his axe, to complete the scene.

The purport of his speech to Captain Maitland, was thanking him, his officers, and ship's company, for the polite attention he had received while on board of the Bellerophon, which he should ever hold in kind remembrance. Something more he would have said after the first pause, and a feeling of deep emotion laboured in his face, and swelled his breast, he looked earnestly in Maitland's face for a moment, as if he was about to renew his speech, but utterance seemed denied; and, slightly moving his hat in salutation, he turned to Savary and Lallemand, who were not allowed to accompany him to St Helena, and spoke to them for a few minutes. What a horrid gloom overhung the ship: had his execution been about to take place there could not have prevailed a more dead silence, so much so, that had a pin fallen from one of the tops on the deck, I am convinced it would have been heard; and to anyone who has known the general buzz of one of our seventy-fours, even at the quietest hour, it is a proof how deeply the attention of every man on board must have been riveted. Before leaving the ship he turned to us on the quarter-deck, once more waved his hand in token of adieu, took hold of the man-ropes, and walked down the side, taking his seat in the Northumberland's barge between Lord Keith and Admiral Cockburn.

Even in this hour of hopeless misery, he lost not sight of that indescribable charm by which he won the hearts of men. On looking back to the ship he saw every head, that could get stuck out of a port, gazing after him; even the rough countenances of the men bespoke a sympathy for his cruel fate, and, apparently conscious of their feelings, the exiled chief again lifted his hat, and inclined his head to the gazing ship's company.

Napoleon in 1820 from a drawing made on St Helena by Captain Henry Duncan Dodgin of the 66th Regiment.

Napoleon in 1818, a watercolour painted from life and said to be a very good likeness. It was painted by Lt.-Colonel Basil Jackson of the Staff Corps in St Helena. This was given by the artist to the Countess Bertrand.

Notes

1. Footnote by the original editor, William Kirk Dickson, (1860-1949): Since this narrative was written in the year 1815, it has been proved by Bonaparte's will, that either his attendants were misinformed, or that they, as well as himself, mis-represented the state of his finances, as he left in the hands of Lafitte, the banker, in Paris, a sum of money amounting to the equivalent of nearly £400,000, besides a very considerable sum said to be vested in the American funds.

2. Anne Jean Marie René Savary, 1st Duke of Rovigo, (1774-1833). Savary suffered several months' internment at Malta and was then allowed to leave and he proceeded to Smyrna in Turkey where he settled for a time. Afterwards he travelled about in more or less distress, but finally was allowed to return to France and regained civic rights; later he settled at Rome. Ill-health compelled him to return to France, and he died in Paris in June 1833.

3. François Antoine Charles Lallemand, (1774-1839). In a similar manner to Savary, Lallemand was allowed to leave Malta and travelled to England where he boarded the ship *Triton* at Liverpool. He landed in Boston under the assumed name of General Cotting. In Philadelphia Lallemand became a president of the French Emigrant Association, an organization that gained a grant of four townships in what is now Alabama for a Vine and Olive Colony. There were rumours that Lallemands would try to rescue Napoleon or put his brother Joseph on a throne in South America. The Alabama land grants were sold to finance another colony in Texas. The planned Texas colony, Champ d'Asile—the Field of Asylum—was meant for defeated Napoleonic veterans. Lallemand stated in public that the colony would have military men only for protection; otherwise it would concentrate on agriculture. On 17 December 1817, 150 would-be-settlers sailed from Philadelphia for Galveston, Texas,

where they arrived on 14 January 1818. Lallemand and his brother reached New Orleans, Louisiana on 2 February 1818, gathered new recruits and on 10 March left for Galveston with 120 volunteers. They sailed up the Trinity River to Atascosito where they built two small forts. However, the Mexican governor Antonio Maria Martinez heard about the French, prepared an expedition to the Trinity River and stationed a force at San Marcos to guard against possible attacks. When the French heard about this move, they abandoned Champ d'Asile around 24 July and fled to Galveston. Lallemand abandoned the colony and returned to New Orleans. Jean Lafitte and Amable Humbert helped some of the survivors to return to Louisiana and the rest walked back to New Orleans in August 1818. Lallemand later became a United States citizen. Napoleon left him 100,000 francs in his will and Lallemand used it to cover his debts. After Louis-Philippe restored the old imperial military grades after the July Revolution of 1830, Lallemand returned to France. From 1837-1838, he served as military governor of Corsica. He died in Paris in 1839.

4. Charles Tristan, marquis de Montholon, (1782-1853). Montholon and his wife accompanied Napoleon to St Helena. Napoleon chiefly dictated to Montholon the notes on his career which form a commentary on the events of the first part of his life. Montholon, despite the departure of his wife, stayed on at Longwood to the end of the emperor's life in May, 1821. He then spent many years in Belgium, and in 1840 acted as "chief of staff" in the "expedition" conducted by Louis Napoleon from London to Boulogne. He was condemned to imprisonment at Ham, but was released in 1847 thanks to the efforts of Gourgaud who was then in favour with the administration; he then retired to England and published the *Récits de la captivité de Napoleon a Ste Hélène*. In 1849 he became one of the deputies for the Legislative Assembly under the Second French Republic. There is a theory among those who believe that Napoleon was murdered by poisoning to regard Montholon as the likely suspect.

5. Gaspard, Baron Gourgaud, (1783-1852). Determined to share Napoleon's exile, he sailed with him on HMS *Northumberland* to St Helena. Tiring of the life at Longwood, he decided to leave the island. The comments he made to his English captors helped to convince Hudson Lowe that Napoleon was feigning illness, that he should not be moved from Longwood, and they led indirectly to the expulsion of Napoleon's doctor, Barry Edward O'Meara. Once in London he quickly demonstrated his support for Napoleon by sending letters to the Empress Marie-Louise and to the Emperors of Austria and Russia. In 1840 he joined other survivors of the captivity who returned to St Helena to bring back Napoleon's remains for burial in Paris—*le retour des cendres*. He

soon published his *Campagne de 1815*, in the preparation of which he had had some help from Napoleon; but Gourgaud's *Journal de Ste-Hélène* was not published until 1899. He became a deputy to the Legislative Assembly in 1849.

6. Count Charles Frederic Jules Piontkowski, (1786-1849). Count Piontkowski arrived at St Helena 29 December 1815 and left on 19 October 1816. Lord Rosebery in his work, whilst outlining some basic facts, dismisses him with, "Piontkowski remains a figure of mystery. He was a trooper in the Polish Lancers, who had followed Napoleon to Elba, and had been given a commission in consequence of his fidelity. At a time when the British Government would not allow Gourgaud to take with him his old servant, or Las Cases to be rejoined by his wife, they sent Piontkowski unbidden and unwelcome to join the Emperor... He vanished as suddenly as he came, nine months afterwards, with, apparently, plenty of money." Telling us that "Napoleon openly suspected him of being a spy," Rosebery rejects this; adds "but his appearance and career at Longwood still require elucidation." Frédéric Masson summarised Piontkowski this way: "It is difficult to deal with the mysterious Polish officer Piontkowski who, after accompanying the Emperor from Malmaison to Rochefort, followed him to England and then when all his companions—those not allowed to proceed to St Helena—were deported to Malta, succeeded, it is not known under whose patronage or by what influence, in joining Napoleon, found himself suspected at the same time by the English and the French, and after a stay of some months during which time he remained a riddle, was taken back to England: then, as a reward for his six months' hypothetical devotion, received annuities and assistance by means of which he lived in luxury during nearly fifty years of journeying round Europe. At St Helena no one asked for him, no one enquired about him, no one grieved for him and he was verily a mystery-man for whom, for no conceivable reason, obstacles were removed and orders countermanded. He appeared before the Emperor in a uniform to which he had no right, took firm root, and was tolerated. He was a glib liar, quite useless, and he departed with no better reason than he had for coming. He was probably only a sharper—this individual who pulled the legs of the English Government, Emperor Napoleon, Sardinia, Austria, Russia, and the rest of Europe."

7. Original comment from *Memoirs of an Aristocrat*, George Home, 1838: 'Our new first lieutenant, Mr Andrew Mott, was the best officer I ever saw in charge of a quarter-deck. I often wondered when that man slept, eat, or dressed himself, for he was hardly ever missed from deck, was always fresh and vigorous, and his dress and appearance would, at any time, have done

honour to the queen's drawing-room. Maitland was, withal, rather a little easy-going, and it occurred to me that, knowing his defect in this way, he contrived always to get a tolerable tartar of a first lieutenant, so that between the captain's good nature and the lieutenant's severity, which he occasionally checked and tempered when he thought the lieutenant was likely to exceed bounds, the ship was kept in capital discipline.'

8. This description contradicts Maitland who said: 'His hair was of a very dark brown, nearly approaching to black, and, though a little thin on the top and front, had not a grey hair amongst it.'

9. *The Poor Gentleman* was a comedy by George Colman, (1762-1836), first performed in 1802.

10. This appears to be a further contradiction from Maitland who said: 'He had the patience to remain to the end of the third act, though, when attending the Opera at Paris, he had always retired at the end of the first.' It seems unlikely that three acts would be performed in twenty minutes.

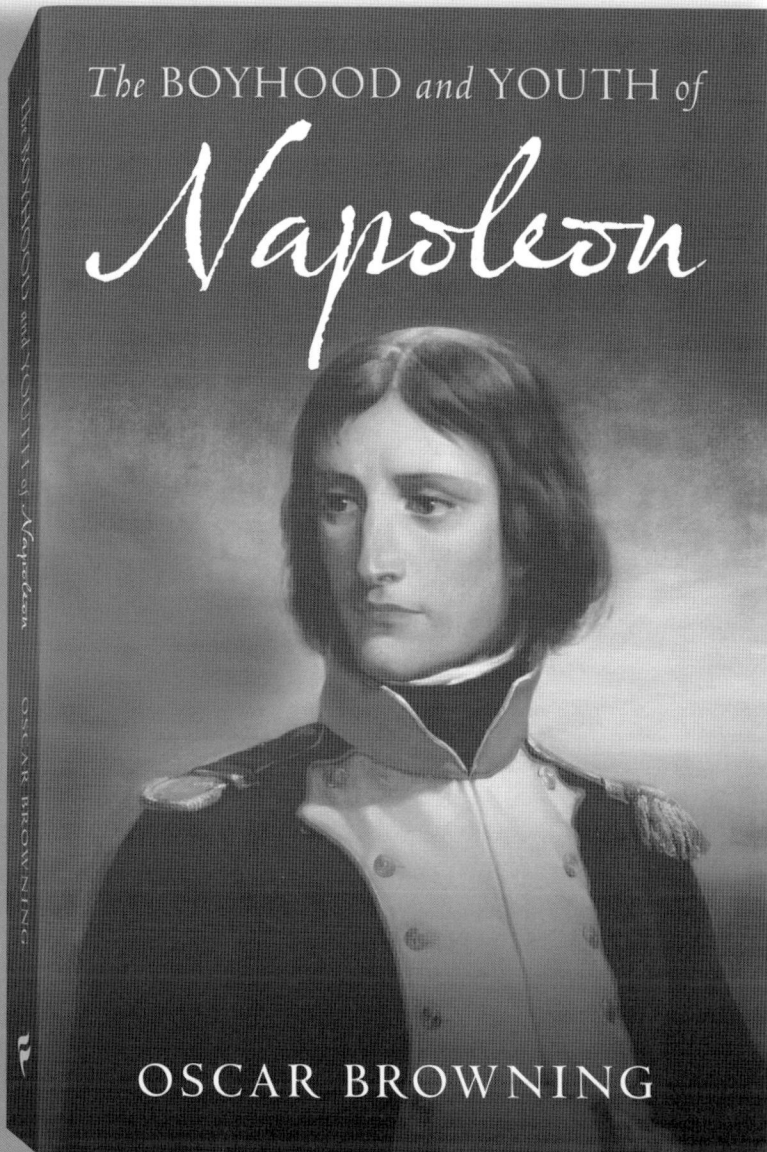

The Boyhood and Youth of Napoleon
ISBN 978-1-78155-011-3 £14.99 $25.95
Paperback 234 x 156mm 176pp 30 illustrations
Available now from www.fonthillmedia.com

Napoleon and His Marshals
ISBN 978-1-78155-036-6 £16.99 $25.95
Paperback 234 x 15mm 256pp 93 illustrations
Available now from www.fonthillmedia.com

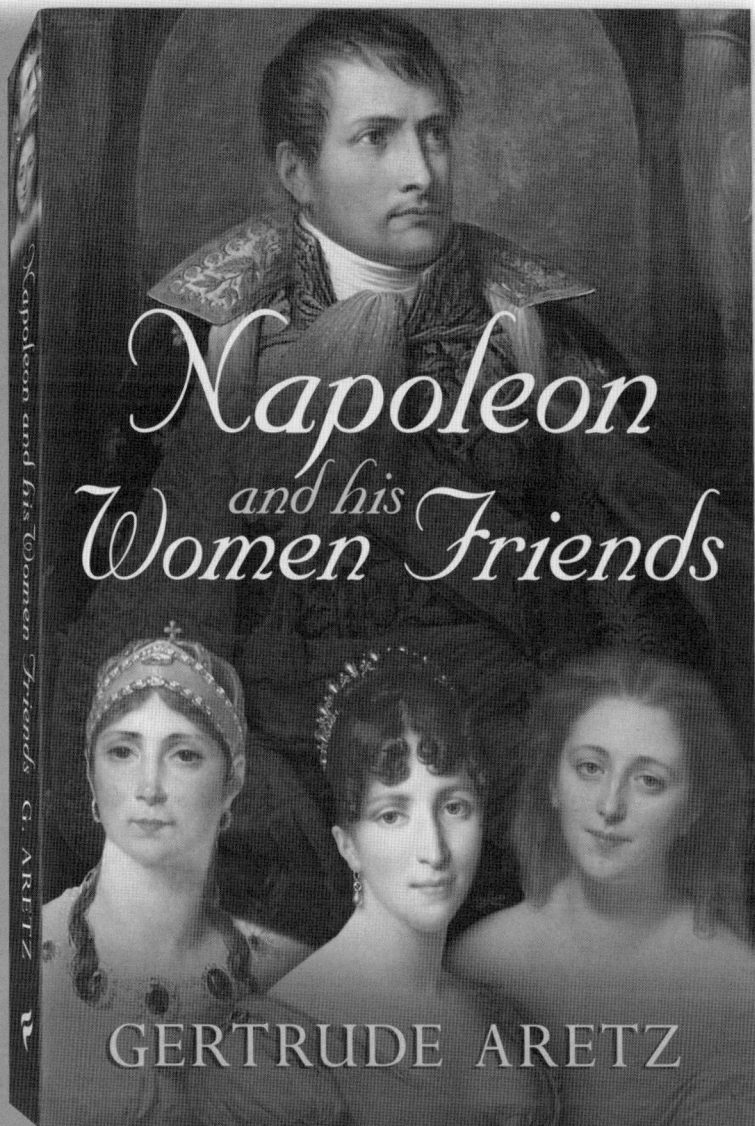

Napoleon and His Women Friends

ISBN 978-1-78155-177-6 £16.9 $25.95

Paperback 234 x 156mm 256pp 98 illustrations

Available now from www.fonthillmedia.com

Napoleon on St Helena

ISBN 978-1-78155-171-4 £16.99 $25.95

Paperback 234 x 156mm 288 79 illustrations, 33 in colour

Available now from www.fonthillmedia.com

Napoleon & Betsy: Recollections of
the Emperor Napoleon on St Helena
ISBN 978-1-78155-034-2 £18.99 $29.95
Hardback 234 x 156mm 176pp 83 illustrations, 33 in colour
Available now from www.fonthillmedia.com

Napoleonic Anecdotes
Anecdotes
LOUIS COHEN

Napoleonic Anecdotes

ISBN 978-1-78155-033-5 £14.99 $21.95

Paperback 234 x 156mm 256pp 32 illustrations

Available now from www.fonthillmedia.com